STUDIES IN THE PERSONAL SOCIAL SERVICES:
NO.2

General editors:
OLIVE STEVENSON and MICHAEL HILL

CHILD ABUSE: ASPECTS OF
INTERPROFESSIONAL CO-OPERATION

Studies in the Personal Social Services

1 SOCIAL WORK AND MONEY
by Michael Hill and Peter Laing

Child Abuse: Aspects of Interprofessional Co-operation

CHRISTINE HALLETT

*Senior Research Fellow, Department of Social Policy and
Social Work
University of Keele*

and

OLIVE STEVENSON

*Professor of Social Policy and Social Work
University of Keele*

London
GEORGE ALLEN & UNWIN
Boston   Sydney

GEORGE ALLEN & UNWIN LTD
40 Museum Street, London WC1A 1LU

© George Allen & Unwin (Publishers) Ltd, 1980

British Library Cataloguing in Publication Data

Hallett, Christine
   Child Abuse.—(Studies in the personal social
   services; 2).
   1. Child abuse services—Great Britain
   I. Title II. Stevenson, Olive
   362.7'1   HV751.A6

ISBN 0-04-362027-2
ISBN 0-04-362028-0 Pbk

Typeset in 10 on 11 point Times by Red Lion Setters, Holborn, London
and printed in Great Britain
by Billing & Sons Ltd, Guildford, London and Worcester

The main aim of the series is to shed light on key areas of concern for the organisation and practice of social work in local authorities. The books are designed for practitioners and for social work students.

The idea for a series of this kind came about from our concern to secure wider discussion of issues which arose during a study of field work in social services departments. This project, funded by the Department of Health and Social Security, the Scottish Social Work Services Group and the Northern Ireland Department of Health and Social Services was directed by Olive Stevenson and Phyllida Parsloe. Its main findings were published by HMSO in *Social Services Teams: The Practitioner's View*. None of the books in this series directly duplicates that report, but some of the issues in them were first discussed there and some of the data quoted in them emerged from that research and may have been reported there.

Olive Stevenson
Michael Hill

Acknowledgements

We are most appreciative of the help received from our colleagues at Keele, Tom Douglas and John Whittaker, concerning the case conference as a small group in social psychological terms. We thank Jill Phillips, our secretary, for her reliable and efficient typing. We are especially grateful to Rowena Tuckwell who has given generously of her spare time in helping with the compilation of the bibliography and the many other details involved in the preparation of a manuscript.

This book is dedicated to the many people in the helping professions who were generous of their time and shared freely with us their experiences and views about inter-professional work.

Contents

Introduction

Although one of the authors wrote about the co-ordination of services for children some fifteen years ago (Stevenson, 1963), this book has its recent origins in our experience of the committee appointed to inquire into the care and supervision provided in relation to Maria Colwell. In our different roles in the inquiry we were privileged to observe, in depth and detail, the workings and, at times, the failings of a complex of welfare services in relation to one child. This, together with subsequent inquiries and government guidance (DHSS, 1974 and DHSS, 1976a), have all emphasised the importance of co-operation between agencies and those who work within them. This book therefore examines inter-organisational and interprofessional relationships, with particular reference to child abuse. It explores some of the difficulties associated with a multi-disciplinary approach and tries to move beyond the exhortatory tone of much of the literature which, while urging inter-disciplinary co-operation, often little explores what might be involved.

The book draws on two separate but related research studies which were sponsored by the Department of Health and Social Security (DHSS). The first is a study of interprofessional communication in case conferences concerning children at risk which we undertook in 1976. In this we observed a small number of case conferences and subsequently interviewed the participants from some of them. The study is described in more detail at the beginning of Chapter 3 and forms the basis for the discussion of the functioning of case conferences in Chapters 3 and 4. A report on this research was published in 1977 (Desborough and Stevenson, 1977).

The second research study on which the book draws is a larger project which took place from 1974-8. This was carried out by the Social Work Research Project (SWRP), of which the authors were members. It examined the task of the local authority field social worker and the implications for social work education and was published in 1978 under the title *Social Service Teams: The Practitioner's View* (DHSS, 1978). As part of this research, the views of members of area teams in social services departments, or their equivalents in Scotland and Northern Ireland, were sought on a number of issues concerned with their work. Three are particularly relevant to this book: the relations between area team staff and other professionals and agencies in the locality; the priorities in work within the teams; and pressures as perceived by the staff. Reference is made to this study throughout the book.

An explanation of the words used in the title seems appropriate. The phrases 'child abuse' or 'child abuse and neglect' have normally been used in the book except where the more narrow and precise term 'non-accidental injury to children' was required. Definitions of child abuse and neglect are many and various. Gil (1970, p. 6), for example, has defined physical abuse as 'the intentional non-accidental use of physical force or intentional non-accidental acts of omission on the part of the parent or other caretaker interacting with the child in his care aimed at hurting, injuring or destroying the child.' However, because the definitions are socially constructed (Gelles and Gelles, 1975), they are constantly being redefined. The past few years have seen a widening of the concept from a concentration on physical injury to a concern with emotional abuse and, more recently, with the sexual abuse of children. For the purposes of this book it is unnecessary to select a single, comprehensive definition. (Such a task may, in any case, be impossible.) The book is concerned with a variety of situations in which one, or many, of the professionals involved considers a child to be at risk of abuse, however defined.

The word 'professionals' has similarly been loosely used: at times as a synonym for those in the human service occupations. We are, of course, aware of the attention paid by sociologists to the concept of professionalism and, more recently, to the process of professionalisation. In Chapter 2 which discusses interprofessional work, reference is made to aspects of this debate concerning, for example, the interprofessional status system and emergent occupational identities. But, for ease of reference, the word 'professionals' has been used in the book to include certain occupational groups, such as the police, who do not display all the attributes normally associated with being a 'profession'.

In our concentration on interprofessional work we risk criticism for ignoring the 'clients' and being more concerned with 'management' and with 'systems' than with helping the children and their families. Although some work on developing and evaluating new modes of treatment is taking place, more is urgently needed. Helping agencies are currently rather better at identifying that abuse may have occurred than at offering appropriate help, whether in prevention or treatment. None the less, even with new types of help, the need for interprofessional work and communication in relation to those families will continue, for they often have multiple problems and may be in contact with many agencies. It is our belief that some understanding of this part of the process will therefore help the children and families concerned. It is also our hope that an understanding of the constraints and opportunities of interprofessional work, which has been gained as a result of the current anxiety and professional investment in child abuse, will usefully be applied in interprofessional work with others, notably the elderly, the handicapped and the mentally ill, whose needs require a concerted response from our fragmented health and welfare services.

Chapter 1

Inter-organisational Relationships – Communications Within and Between Agencies

A recognition that inter-agency co-operation is required to deal with the problem of child abuse is not new. As long ago as 1950 a government circular (Home Office, 1950) on ill-treated children recommended the establishment of children's co-ordinating committees. The detailed scrutiny undertaken by some committees of inquiry into cases of child abuse[1] has, however, recently revealed the range of agencies involved and the complexity of the relationships within and between them. Indeed, the committee of inquiry into the provision and co-ordination of services to the family of John George Auckland (Auckland report, 1975, p. 13) describes the services provided to that family as 'a demonstration of how the Welfare State operates' (p. 13)—although many failures were revealed.

Most of the agencies which may be involved are public bodies with a variety of organisational structures. They include the national health service, with hospital and community based services and the school health service; social services departments with field, residential and day care services; education departments including schools, the education welfare service and the educational psychologists; housing departments, sometimes including housing welfare services; the probation service; the prison service, including the prison medical service; the police; local authority legal services usually provided by the county secretary's department; the social security system, and so on. In addition, voluntary agencies, notably the National Society for the Prevention of Cruelty to Children (NSPCC) and the Royal Scottish Society for the Prevention of Cruelty to Children (RSSPCC), Family Service Units (FSUs), Family Welfare Agency (FWA) and voluntary playgroups may be involved. Not all agencies are active in every case and simply to list some of the possible combinations illustrates the size of the inter-organisational task.

Some of the services are provided by local authorities, with the complication that, following local government reorganisation in 1974, housing is provided in the non-metropolitan counties at district level, while social services, education and legal services are at county council level. Other services, such as the prison service or social security, for example, are directly provided or more tightly controlled by central government. Thus inter-organisational communication has to take place between agencies with very varied structures as well as different powers, duties, objectives, traditions, work styles and value systems. Furthermore, many of them have recently been reorganised.

An awareness of the inter-relatedness of many social problems, not only child abuse, coupled with a desire to maximise resources through co-ordinated planning and delivery of service, has powerfully influenced the recent organisational changes in the health and personal social services. At central government level it was one of the reasons for combining in 1968 in the DHSS responsibility for the social security system, the national health service, and the local authority personal social services under the Secretary of State for Social Services. The Seebohm Committee (Cmnd 3703, 1968, p. 44) in recommending the creation of unified social services departments from the former local authority children's, health and welfare departments, anticipated that 'they would ensure a more co-ordinated and comprehensive approach to the problems of individuals and families and the community in which they live.' Similarly, the reorganisation of the national health service in 1974 aimed to improve its internal co-ordination through the integration of hospitals with some community health services. The establishment (outside London) of area health authorities with boundaries coterminous, wherever possible, with those of the reorganised local authorities, reflected the importance attached to co-operation between the services. This was reinforced by a statutory requirement to establish machinery, joint consultative committees, to promote effective co-operation between health and social services.[2]

The report of the committee of inquiry into the care and supervision provided in relation to Maria Colwell (Colwell report, 1974), however, notes that in terms of improved communication and co-ordination, the committee considered that the Seebohm reorganisation, with its aim of 'one door on which to knock' had little altered Maria's case. The Auckland report (1975, p. 92) went further in commenting on the detrimental effects in that case of these reorganisations:

We recognise that those who advocate drastic reorganisations in public services often foresee great benefits and sometimes great benefits do result. But there is also nearly always great disruption, which careful planning may reduce but cannot eliminate. The disruption, although well-known, is rarely emphasised, but in this case it almost certainly contributed to depriving a child of supervision and support that were literally vital.

Clearly the outcome of such major reorganisation of services must be decided in the longer term and by taking account of other criteria. It is, however, salutary to note the disruptive effects, even if only temporary, on service delivery and this is particularly pertinent as plans for devolving responsibility for the provision of social services to some district councils are under active consideration.[3]

Three levels of co-ordination between welfare agencies have been identified by Reid (1964) and Carter (1976) has applied them to child abuse. The first, *'ad hoc* case co-ordination', describes the variety of contacts by letter, telephone or face-to-face discussion between practitioners about particular cases. The second level, 'systematic case co-ordination', is seen in case conferences which are examined in Chapters 3 and 4. The third, 'programme co-ordination', is partly seen in area review committees—the inter-agency committees for local policy making about child abuse and neglect.

If arrangements for co-ordinating inter-agency services for children have their origins in the circular issued in 1950, their development in relation to child abuse continued in the 1960s with the increased awareness of the problem of the 'battered baby' following the pioneering work of Kempe (1962). In 1966, for example, the DHSS and the Home Office circulated a memorandum about 'battered babies' prepared by the British Paediatric Association for field authorities. In 1970 Children's Officers and Medical Officers of Health were asked in a letter from the DHSS and the Home Office (DHSS and Home Office, 1970) to hold local consultations with interested agencies to review the local situation and decide what further arrangements should be made to ensure that protection and assistance were made available to the child, others at risk in the family and to the parents and other adults. The letter asked for a progress report on the local consultations and in 1972 the DHSS reported (DHSS, 1972) that most areas had in existence a review committee to plan local policy and management and to co-operate with adjacent areas.

This was the stage of development when the main letter of guidance on the subject was issued in 1974 (DHSS, 1974). Now more appropriately entitled 'non-accidental injury to children', the letter began:

Although we realise how busy you are with reorganisation, recent events have left us in no doubt of the need to repeat the professional guidance about the diagnosis, care, prevention and local organisation necessary for the management of cases of non-accidental injury to children.

In their written evidence to the Select Committee on Violence in the Family (HC 329-III, 1977), the DHSS indicate that perhaps the most important of the 'recent events' was the case of Maria Colwell, and the publicity it attracted. They state (p. 454):

the need for improved communication between the many services involved, which was known to have caused concern to the Committee inquiring into the case of Maria Colwell even before their Report was received in the Department in late April 1974, was taken into account in preparing the guidance issued earlier that month.

The guidance concerning the framework for inter-agency relationships contained three main recommendations: first, that where they did not already exist, area review committees should be formed in each local authority/area health authority as policy making bodies for the management of cases of child abuse; secondly, that a case conference should be held for every case involving suspected non-accidental injury to a child, and thirdly, that consideration be given to setting up a register of cases.

The main functions of area review committees are devising and advising on procedures for dealing with cases, reviewing the work of case conferences and providing education and training programmes for staff dealing with cases. The committees are characterised by wide membership and the letter of guidance recommended representation at 'senior level' from four departments of the local authority (social services, chief executive, education and housing) from fourteen branches of the health service (primary and specialist health care teams, and nursing, dental and medical administration) as well as the police, the probation service and the NSPCC.

An interesting feature of the systems of area review committees and case conferences devised to diagnose and manage cases of child abuse is that they are non-statutory. For example, in marked contrast to the position in the USA, authorities are not required by law to maintain registers of children at risk. The relevant letter (DHSS, 1974, p. 5) simply states: 'Area Review Committees should give urgent consideration to setting up within existing resources an adequate system in their area for this purpose.' In part this non-legislative response by central government may just be seen as a continuation of the style of relationship which the Ministry of Health (as the predecessor of the DHSS) had with health and welfare authorities, described by Brown (1975) as *'laissez-faire'* in contrast to the more directive 'paternalistic' role of the Home Office *vis-à-vis* children's departments. An example of this is the contrast between the statutory framework for the provision of services to the elderly, as contained in the National Assistance Act 1948, and the volume of legislation and close regulation of services for children issued from the Home Office, such as the Boarding Out Regulations, 1955.[4] Another illustration is the change in function from the concern of the Home Office Children's Inspectorate with monitoring standards of practice to the advisory rather than the inspectorial role of the Social Work Service located in the DHSS (Utting, 1978).

It is, however, likely that the measures which are periodically required to ensure or facilitate inter-agency co-operation—the sanction of the law, for example, or increased resources recently provided for joint funding initiatives between health and social services—were not necessary in relation to the management of child abuse cases. For it seems that 'external forces in the environment', identified by Davidson (1976) as important variables in the development of inter-organisational relationships, were propitious. In particular, public and professional anxiety were a powerful impetus to inter-agency co-ordination, and the public exposure likely to follow a tragedy perhaps an effective sanction. This may be as important as Lupton's suggestion (1977, p. 143) that it was the recognition that area review committees were 'the only forum in which the necessary meeting of minds and reconciliation of policies between authorities, agencies and professions can be sought', which provided the impetus to their establishment and to the progress that was made. A suggestion that more powerful factors were operating would help to explain why, in the view expressed by the Association of Directors of Social Services to the Select Committee on Violence in the Family, 'a letter of guidance from central government has had more effect in moulding the development of services and shifting resources than a major piece of legislation such as the Chronically Sick and Disabled Persons Act, or even the Children and Young Persons Act' (HC 329-III, 1977, p. 632).

Davidson (1976, p. 120) has proposed a typology of inter-organisational relationships as follows:

If two or more agencies are communicating, they are doing no more than talking together, sharing information, ideas, and feelings about the shape of their shared world. When mere communication leads to the suggestion that organisations 'work together' on some small project, they may be said to be co-operating. This stage is characterised by informality of the arrangements and a degree of vagueness of the tasks to be accomplished or even of the broader goals to be achieved. When the arrangements become more formalised and the tasks more clearly limited and well-defined, the nature of the relations may be thought of as a confederation, still loose and without formal sanctions for non-participation. When the organisations are willing to define the goals and tasks precisely and to create a formal structure to carry them out and when they are willing to cede a degree of their autonomy to that joint structure, a federation exists. When the structure is formalised to the point that the original organisations are willing to give up their identities as organisations, as least regarding the specific domain(s) in which the co-operation has occurred, they may decide to merge, to form a new formal organisation.

A feature of Davidson's scheme is that the boundaries of the differing stages may overlap as inter-organisational relationships change and develop. Applying the scheme to area review committees, it is clear that they have some characteristics of confederation and some of federation—still of the former in that there are no *formal* sanctions for non-participation and not wholly of the latter because the extent to which autonomy has been ceded, if at all, varies from agency to agency. This is illustrated in that, notwithstanding participation in the area review committees and multidisciplinary case conferences, certain agencies, notably the police, NSPCC and social services departments, often explicitly reserve the right to take independent action.

There seems to be a consensus that, in general, area review committees have performed valuable functions particularly in developing guidance for the management of cases, establishing register systems, organising training days on non-accidental injury and increasing interprofessional understanding at senior levels.[5]

However, some problems in their functioning have been identified, particularly in London where local authority and area health authority boundaries are not co-terminous—a situation which can result in particularly complex and strained relationships. The main criticism is that the committees are cumbersome, top-heavy and 'over-bureaucratised'. The Select Committee on Violence in the

Family therefore recommended: 'that, now the general conscious-
ness of non-accidental injury has been greatly increased, the
elaborate structure of Area Review Committee should be kept
under constant review with the aim of simplifying it and making it
less expensive in terms of manpower' (HC 329-I, 1977, p. xxxi).
Apart from recommending that quarterly meetings should take
place, the government does not suggest how business should be
conducted. The committees could devise their own ways of organising business. Thus some have set up sub-committees and *ad hoc*
working parties, which are more economical of staff time.

Another problem, seen also in inter-organisational contacts at
other levels of co-ordination, particularly in the case conferences, is
more fundamental and occurs when members speak with differing
degrees of authority for the agencies or professional interests they
represent. This is related, in part, to the place that representatives
on the committee occupy in their own internal agency hierarchy
and the degree of delegated authority they can exercise. Some members will be able to commit their agency, others will not. Other members, while representing particular professional interests, cannot
necessarily speak for or commit their colleagues. This is illustrated
particularly clearly with reference to general practitioners who have
managed, despite the reorganisation of the national health service, to retain their somewhat 'free-floating position' as independent
contractors to Family Practitioner Committees. The report of the
joint committee of inquiry into non-accidental injury to children,
with particular reference to the case of Lisa Godfrey (Lisa Godfrey
report, 1975, p. 34) highlighted the difficulties, referring to the 'need
for considerable improvement in the communication of information to the family practitioner service' and to the problem of
'integrating them in arrangements set up by area review committees'.

One of the tasks assigned to area review committees was setting
up local register systems to aid communication between the disciplines involved. The government did not institute a legal duty of
reporting child abuse, thereby avoiding having to define precisely
the form and circumstances in which reports to registers should be
made. The 1974 letter did not, therefore, specify how the registers
should be organised and the local exercise of discretion has resulted
in register systems which vary widely from area to area. The DHSS
inquiries reported in the 1976 letter (DHSS, 1976a) and the British
Association of Social Workers (BASW) working party report *The
Central Child Abuse Register* (BASW, 1978) both confirm great
variety in, for example, the criteria for registration and de-registra-
tion, the amount of information recorded and arrangements for
access to the register.

Four main purposes of registers can be distinguished. One is to aid the diagnosis of cases by recording previous professional concern so that those workers whose suspicion is aroused—health visitors, social workers, teachers or doctors and nurses in accident and emergency departments—may check whether the child is known, or suspected, to be at risk. A second purpose is to provide a source of epidemiological data for statistical and research purposes about identified and registered cases in any locality. A third, related to the management of child abuse, is to use the register to identify the cases requiring review at specified intervals, often dependent on the category of registration, whether, for example, 'known to be injured', 'suspected of being injured', or 'at risk of being injured'. The reviews may be carried out by area review committees or their sub-committees, by NSPCC Special Units where these exist, or by individual agencies. A fourth purpose is concerned with allocation of resources, for it appears that, in certain areas, being 'on the register' is a key to scarce resources, such as a playgroup place (BASW, 1978, p. 30).

Several problems have resulted from the existence of these varied and multi-purpose registers. One crucial problem centring on the criteria for registration concerns the tension between registers which are sufficiently large to be useful as an aid to early diagnosis and yet small enough to be manageable. The 1976 circular of guidance from the DHSS stated only that details of injured children under 16 should be recorded and that 'in deciding on criteria for the inclusion of "at risk" cases authorities should consider how to ensure that children believed to be in the greatest danger will be recorded without entailing an unrealistic workload in the review of cases.' If registers are to be used to help professional decision making at the diagnostic stage they would function most effectively in *this* respect if minor and unconfirmed suspicions were recorded. The BASW working party (1978, p. 37) states one of the purposes of registers to be 'to protect a child by recording the concern expressed by a group of professionals' and continues:

the child likely to be at risk of repeated abuse is the one where isolated incidents of abuse go unnoticed so that no pattern is seen. A child injured in the past may show no obvious signs of trauma but on the evidence of past abuse a worker may make a different diagnosis when confronted by a further suspicious injury, if that evidence is available . . .

The use of registers in this way was illustrated in the case conference study by a social worker who had been called to the local accident and emergency department to see a child with minor, although clearly non-accidental, injuries. The family was well-known to the social services department as a 'problem family' but there was no previous known history of physical ill treatment. The father admitted injuring the child, following his persistent bed-wetting and, as the case was considered to be an isolated incident of over-chastisement, the social worker had in the circumstances decided to allow the child to return home. None the less, at the case conference the social worker argued strongly that the family should be registered so that any duty social worker or other professional would have available information about the incident if further injuries occurred. There was strong opposition to this suggestion, with some participants arguing that duty social workers should take decisions on the information confronting them in such situations and not rely on the register. Furthermore, in this case, registration was considered by some to be a too 'serious' step. The social worker explained that, in her view, when making decisions in such situations it was not a case of 'relying' on the register but rather of gathering the available information to enable any decision to be as informed as possible.

If, however, suspected cases were to be more freely notified to the register in less clear-cut circumstances, three important issues are raised.

One concerns civil liberties. The rights of parents to be told, the possibility of appeal against 'wrongful' registration and the criteria for removal are important matters even if much stricter criteria are required for registration; but the risk of infringements in this respect is greater if the merest suspicion on the part of any professional can result in registration. It is possible that large lists recording unsubstantiated and vague professional concern, particularly about the possibility of 'risk' rather than the recording of injuries, would lead to widespread public and professional disquiet and to the discrediting of the registers.

A second issue is that a large register of this type is likely to be inaccurate and difficult to review and keep up to date. This is undoubtedly so although a simple system of removal of names after a specified period, if no further inquiries about the family were made, might help.

The third issue raised is the usefulness or appropriateness of widespread registration as a professional response to suspected child abuse. It could be argued that registering large numbers of cases on the merest suspicion lets professionals 'off the hook' of a more rigorous assessment of the degree of risk and a decision as to whether preventive or other work might be necessary.

Currently, the local discretion about criteria for registration has important consequences. The use of registers for gathering national information about the incidence of abuse or simple data about the age of children involved is strictly limited while the criteria vary so widely from authority to authority. Also, the significance of registration and particularly of being in a certain category on the register is sometimes not understood within authorities (see Chapter 4). Equally important, the uncertainty can cause difficulties when families move from one area to another with more or less liberal registration policies. For example, the report of the committee of inquiry concerning Simon Peacock (Simon Peacock report, 1978, p. 17) states that the decision to place the child in the 'suspected' category on the register was one of the contributory factors whereby the 'alert' failed to sound as effectively as it might have done when the family moved to a neighbouring authority. The committee conclude 'it may be desirable to review the method of dividing the register, to guard against a false sense of security being engendered by names being registered in lower categories of risk.'

In practice, it seems that many registers combine the primary functions of being a guide to management of cases of abuse and an aid to diagnosis. Some contain only the names of children with proven non-accidental injuries, while others include suspected physical injuries, emotional abuse and often a catch-all 'at risk' category. The Select Committee on Violence in the Family recommended that there should be two-tier registers with separate categories for injured children and those 'at risk' and state: 'we have asked that the register include a wide category of 'at risk' children where a case conference (i.e. before registration) would not be appropriate' (HC 329-I, 1977, p. xxxiii). The BASW working party report on registers rejected this view and considered that children should be either 'on' or 'off' the register. Their recommendations, that names should only be placed on the register following a case conference, that monitoring of work done should be linked to the register and that only 'severe' and 'persistent' cases of emotional abuse should be recorded, indicate that they wish the register to be a list of serious cases in which interprofessional work is already under way.

The government, in the White Paper *Violence to Children* (Cmnd 7123, 1978) issued in response to the Select Committee's report, undertook to issue guidance to ensure greater standardisation in register systems, adding 'these are, however, matters on which there is a variety of views, many of them conflicting . . .' (p. 16). The arguments are finely balanced. Perhaps the most urgent need is for clarification one way or the other to end the present diversity and confusion.

The 1974 letter of guidance asked area review committees to 'approve written instructions defining the duties of all personnel concerned with any aspect of these cases'. The instructions, which provide the framework for local management of individual cases, are normally issued in procedural handbooks for staff, and since they are drafted locally they vary in style and content from one area to another. Much of their emphasis is on communication and thus inter-organisational and intra-organisational relationships concerning children at risk are distinctive in the degree to which they are governed by procedural guidance. The following extract from one area review committee's procedures appended to the 1976 circular (DHSS, 1976a), concerning action to be taken by community nursing staff in cases where there is a strong suspicion of non-accidental injury, is a typical example of the precision and detail of such advice:

(1) Nursing staff should inform the General Practitioner and telephone the Senior Nursing Officer (Community) immediately, giving full details of the case.

(2) This should be followed, within twenty-four hours, by a written report to the Senior Nursing Officer (Community). In the event of non-availability of the Senior Nursing Officer, staff should contact the Nursing Officer (Health Visiting).

(3) On receiving the information, the Senior Nursing Officer should contact the District Controller for Social Services and, if necessary, the Consultant Paediatrician.

(4) Referral of cases to Social Services District Centres should take place on the same day that suspicion is aroused.

(5) Copies of the reports from field workers should be sent via the Senior Nursing Officer to the District Community Physician and the Specialist in Community Medicine (Social Services) within twenty-four hours. (A copy of this report should be retained by the Senior Nursing Officer.)

(6) The form for inclusion in the Central Register of Non-Accidental Injury, should be forwarded via the Senior Nursing Officer to the Area Nurse/Child Health within seventy-two hours.

(7) Follow-up reports on all cases included in the Register of Non-Accidental Injury to Children, which in future will be called the Central Register, will be requested by the Area Nurse (Child Health) every three months.

Guidance of this kind can help to overcome a major problem in inter- and intra-agency communication—that of knowing who, and

at what level, to contact when about what. Problems caused by
uncertainty over this have been highlighted elsewhere in this series
by Hill and Laing (1979) in relation to social workers and supplementary benefits officials and, with reference to links between
education and the social services, by Davie (1977). It is also a
common complaint that 'following Seebohm' GPs have found it
difficult to make appropriate contacts with the larger social services
departments, particularly since the intake or duty officers' rota
systems often mean that referrals are dealt with by different people.
Procedural guidance has, then, helped to clarify this part of the
process of communication, although there is still some evidence
that problems can arise from the distortions or delays which may
occur as communications go 'up and over' the hierarchy, as the
following extract from the Simon Peacock report (1978, p. 12)
illustrates:

> On 19 November a formal notification was sent from Suffolk
> Social Services Department to the Director of Social Services at
> Shire Hall, Cambridge, to confirm that Simon, who was on the
> Non-Accidental Injury Register, had moved. The Cambridge-
> shire procedures indicate that the notification should be sent to
> the co-ordinator but in this case it was sent direct to the Director
> of Social Services at Cambridge. The letter arrived on 23
> November and was *sent* to the co-ordinator, based elsewhere in
> Cambridge, reaching her on 2 December.

The co-ordinator had, in this case, apparently acted before receiving the letter and there had previously been direct contact between
the field workers involved in the authorities so the delay was not
material. The extract is quoted simply to show how easily a
fourteen-day delay in communication can occur.

Procedural guidelines such as these have engendered a good deal
of controversy concerning their value or appropriateness for professional staff. They strike at the heart of the continuing and, at
times, oversimplified debate about the tension between professional responsibility and organisational accountability, or, as it is
more usually expressed, between 'professionals' and 'bureaucracies'. Etzioni (1969, p. x) writes:

> Only if immune from ordinary social pressures and free to inno-
> vate, to experiment, to take risks without the usual social reper-
> cussions of failure can a professional carry out his work
> effectively. It is this highly individualised principle which is
> diametrically opposed to the very essence of the organisational

principle of control and co-ordination by superiors. In other words, the ultimate justification for a professional act is that it is, to the best of the professional's knowledge, the right act . . . The ultimate justification of an administrative act, however, is that it is in line with the organisation's rules and regulations, and that it has been approved—directly or by implication—by a superior rank.

To make such a sharp dichotomy between professional and bureaucratic norms seems inappropriate when many professionals—teachers, nurses, doctors, social workers—are employed within large organisations. Indeed, these organisations actually enable some professionals to follow their chosen occupations. Private social work practice is, in this country, still very insignificant and who ever heard of a private health visitor? In addition, many professionals spend a substantial part of their training undertaking practical work in the type of organisations which subsequently employ them, whether schools, hospitals, or social services departments. Thus, as Toren (1969, p. 151) suggests, the students undergo 'a process of anticipatory socialisation to the role of professional in a bureaucratic organisation'. The third complication to so sharp a distinction is the extent to which the bureaucracies have themselves become professionalised. This can be seen, for example, in the professionally dominated multi-disciplinary management systems devised in the reorganised national health service, and also in the numbers of professionally qualified senior staff in management roles within social services departments. Thus much, although not all, of the control exercised within these organisations is by senior members of a professional group over its junior members. These observations are not to suggest that large organisations are, by definition, always helpful and congenial to those employed in professional roles within them, but rather to agree with Hill (1972, p. 161) that 'insofar as there is conflict which may be crudely described as "professionals versus bureaucracy" the ethical arguments are not nearly as one-sided as those who see organisational employment as a threat to freedom have tried to suggest.'

The response to the child abuse procedures needs to be located within this wider debate. There are four main criticisms: that they are too time-consuming and cumbersome; that they encourage over-reaction and a tendency to 'play safe'; that they remove professional discretion; and that, with their focus on administrative procedures, they serve to protect the agency rather than the interests of the child and family.[6]

It may be somewhat ingenuous to blame the child abuse

procedures themselves for the anxiety which undoubtedly exists
and for some over-reaction or reluctance to take risks. It seems
more appropriate to view the procedures as an understandable
response to the public and professional anxiety which preceded
them and contributed to their development. Menzies has analysed
the organisation of hospital nursing services in terms of their
functioning as a social system which provides a defence against
anxiety. Two facets of this study are particularly significant in considering child abuse procedures. The first concerns the response to
the anxiety which stems from having to take decisions in the
absence of full information about the consequences of the choice.
Menzies (1970, p. 15) writes:

> All decisions are thus necessarily attended by some uncertainty
> about their outcome and consequently by some conflict and
> anxiety, which will last until the outcome is known ... To spare
> staff such anxiety, the nursing service attempts to minimise the
> number and variety of decisions that must be made. Precise
> instructions are given about the way each task be performed, the
> order of the tasks and the time for the performance although
> such precise instructions are not objectively necessary, or even
> wholly desirable.

The other is that in the face of considerable change and strain on
staffing within the hospital, which seemed to require a flexible
response, the difficulties were handled 'by increased prescription
and rigidity and by reiteration of the familiar. As far as one could
gather, the greater the anxiety the greater the need for such reassur-
ance in rather compulsive repetition' (p. 23). Similar tendencies to
prescribe and similar rigidity in the face of anxiety can be seen in
the procedures developed in relation to child abuse.

Procedural guidance can, however, offer protection to staff, to
the agencies which employ them and to clients in several ways.

First, by spelling out more clearly than has generally been the
case, the nature of shared responsibility and decision making
within organisations which are bureaucratically structured, such as
hospitals, schools, and social services departments. Most of the
procedures, for example, first define duties of basic grade workers
in these cases, in particular which staff at senior level they should
inform, and then spell out the responsibilities of senior staff. This
helps to clarify some of the confusion about the relationship
between organisational accountability and personal and professional responsibility.

The handbooks can also help to protect clients and ensure at least a minimum level of service, for example, by serving as valuable *aides-memoires* and providing some structure for field staff and those in supervisory roles in busy working weeks when the child abuse cases may constitute only a small proportion of a heavy and demanding workload. With their emphasis on multi-disciplinary management and review of cases, the procedures may serve as a restraining influence on over-involvement on the part of the key, or other, worker. Also, if the required standards of work are clearly spelled out, it is easier to demonstrate to management when resources in staff time or skill are inadequate for implementation.

Finally, procedures can offer protection when things go wrong. There is likely to be a continuing need to examine particular cases by means of various forms of inquiry or internal review when it seems that there are lessons to be learned or that there have been serious professional failings. In these circumstances those who have followed the agency rules should be more protected than some of their predecessors facing committees of inquiry when, far from the *required* professional standards being clear, there was uncertainty even about what could be considered appropriate standards of work and responses in certain circumstances. The corollary is that those who have fallen short may be vulnerable.

None the less, despite the help which can be offered by procedural guidance there is some substance in the criticisms made. A central one is that with their concentration on non-accidental injury, rather than physical and emotional abuse of children, or more widely still, on work to improve the quality of life of young children and their parents, the procedures have played their part in setting and, it may be argued, distorting priorities within the helping professions. But the procedures themselves only account in part for this.

It is difficult to assess the specific contribution made by the procedures, as distinct from other factors, to the high level of professional anxiety in cases of child abuse. Much anecdotal evidence exists that individual workers may have 'over-reacted' in particular cases. In the case conference study, for example, there were references to two occasions when place of safety orders had been taken in a manner which some conference participants considered to have been hasty and ill-judged. The Association of Directors in their evidence to the Select Committee on Violence in the Family reported that there had been a 'great increase' in the anxiety levels of staff with a tendency to act defensively in non-accidental injury cases.

The authors' postal questionnaire survey of the numbers of case conferences called in local authorities in the United Kingdom in two consecutive months in 1976 suggested that professional anxiety may vary widely from area to area, and indeed from district to district. The survey, which had a 95 per cent response rate, revealed very wide variations in the numbers of case conferences called in the period under review. For example, a London borough held over a hundred conferences, a rate of one per some 2,500 population, while another held only one conference, one per some 200,000 people. Eleven authorities held over sixty conferences in the two months, at least one every working day, while, at the other extreme, sixteen authorities held under ten.

The numbers of conferences called were not related to such basic data as, for example, the population served, the numbers of children under 18 or the numbers of children in care. These wide differences can be explained, in part, by different local procedures concerning the criteria for registration of cases and the arrangements for the holding of case conferences and for review of cases. The differences in procedural guidance may themselves reflect the degree of local professional anxiety at area review committee level. But it is probable that the variations in the numbers of conferences held are also related to the differing anxiety levels of the field staff who implement the procedures.

Other indicators exist which may suggest, if not high anxiety, at least greater caution on the part of professional staff. The table opposite shows the sharp increase in the number of place of safety orders in force to local authorities at 31 March for the years 1972 to 1976.

The number of care orders made in the years 1972 to 1976 is also of interest. While the numbers of children committed to care because they had committed offences showed little variation, the numbers of children committed under other sections of the 1969 Children and Young Persons Act increased from 4,000 in 1972 to 6,400 in 1976 (HC 506, 1977, p. 5).

One explanation for the rise in the number of place of safety orders and care orders may simply be that the professionals, as well as magistrates and the public, are more alert and better informed about the problem of child abuse and neglect and are therefore recognising and dealing with more cases. Another is that the emphasis placed by the DHSS letter (1974) and local guidance on the need to consider seeking place of safety orders is likely to have affected practice in this respect. An additional explanation is that the rise in both care orders and place of safety orders is a reflection of professional anxiety and a tendency to 'play safe'.

Further empirical work is required to ascertain whether undue occupational anxiety exists which might be reflected, for example,

Date	Numbers of place of safety orders*
March 1972	204
March 1973	214
Maria Colwell Inquiry sitting ---	
March 1974	353
Publication of Maria Colwell Report ---	
March 1975	596
March 1976	759

*In force to local authorities at 31 March 1972–6.

in higher sickness rates (Menzies, 1970) or whether the increases reflect appropriately increased levels of concern and caution amongst professional staff and magistrates. However, since, as Rowe states (1977a, p. 556), it cannot be assumed 'that alternative forms of care are either regularly or readily available in all areas or indeed that they can necessarily provide a happy and satisfactory alternative to family life whether this be temporarily or permanently', it is important to ensure that such actions are taken in the interests of the child and not primarily because those involved have not been helped to manage the anxiety and take the risks inherent in work of this kind.

The influence of procedures on the exercise of professional discretion is complex. In some respects they do limit the choice of action open to workers in that they are instructed to make particular responses to certain situations, for example, the circumstances in which medical examination must be sought. However, the procedures do not and cannot remove the need for the exercise of professional judgement. A crucial point at which discretion is exercised, for example, is in the initial stage when individual workers are responding to what they have observed or to referrals made to them in deciding whether they suspect a child to be at risk and thus whether the procedures should be brought into operation. Particularly difficult are the so-called 'grey areas' on the margins of abuse, where there may be ill-defined anxiety about the quality of parenting or doubt about where the line between over-chastisement and non-accidental injury should be drawn. Area review committees vary in the precision with which they have defined the cases to which the procedures should apply. In all cases, however, even when the criteria are tightly drawn, workers must exercise judgement about when to air their suspicions. It has been suggested (BASW, 1978, p. 32) that some workers may be reluctant to raise doubts about the possibility of child abuse because of the consequences of activating the 'complex multi-agency procedures' over which *they* have little control.

It is important that these procedures are revised as knowledge increases and treatment skills develop. It has, for example, become a widely accepted principle that immediate hospital admission is required for injured children. The DHSS letter of guidance (1974, p. 1) states: 'When there is reasonable suspicion of non-accidental injury the child should at once be admitted to hospital for diagnosis and for his own safety. Anything less would expose him to unacceptable risk.' Social workers have been surprisingly slow in pointing out the attendant dangers, but more attention is now being focused on the *needs* of the abused child (for example, Okell Jones, 1977). Martin, a developmental paediatrician, has written (1977, p. 16):

> We must consider the iatrogenic effect of our well-meaning treatment plans. Far too often, our treatment plans have added more stress for the child to cope with. What happens when physical abuse is recognised? We hospitalise the child even though there may be no medical indications and the child must cope with the deleterious effects of the hospital environment. We separate the child from his parents, parents who, even though abusive, do represent caring people for the child.

Such thinking has led the Tunbridge Wells Study Group to reconsider its original resolution that hospital admission was required, and the group now believes that admission to hospital may not always be absolutely necessary. They suggest (in Franklin, 1977a, p. 183) that protection for the child might be ensured in less traumatic ways, for example, by placing the child with previously known foster parents or, rarely, by leaving the child at home with suitable help. The important point here is that the necessity for hospital admission is now enshrined in procedural guidance for practitioners. There is usually a time-lag between 'research' and new thinking about treatment and its effect on day-to-day practice but the very existence of procedures may slow down this process in the field of child abuse.

It is clear that there is greater certainty about making decisions that children have been or are at risk of abuse than there is about how most appropriately to offer help to the children and their families. Work on developing, implementing and evaluating treatment programmes is in progress here and elsewhere, for example, Helfer and Kempe (1968 and 1976), Kempe and Helfer (1972), Baher *et al.* (1976) and Schmitt (1978). It is not perhaps surprising that, to date, procedural guidance has concentrated on inter- and intra-agency communication rather than on treatment skills, particularly since the importance of interprofessional communication in these cases seems incontrovertible.

NOTES

1 c.f. in particular the following reports: Colwell, Auckland, Lisa Godfrey and Karen Spencer.
2 NHS Reorganisation Act 1973, Section 10.
3 *House of Commons Parliamentary Debates* Vol. 955, Issue No. 1118, cols. 752-4, 2-3 August 1978 (HMSO, London, 1978).
4 The Boarding Out of Children Regulations, 1955 (No. 1377, S.I. 1955).
5 c.f., for example, *Select Committee on Violence in the Family* HC 329-I, p. xxxi (1977).
6 c.f., for example, Popplestone, R. 'Moving the balance from administration to practice', *Social Work Today* vol. 8, no. 13, 1977; and *Select Committee on Violence in the Family*, HC 329-II, 1977, p. 250 and HC 329-III, 1977, p. 515.

Chapter 2

Interprofessional Work

The preceding chapter discussed the arrangements for structuring inter-organisational relationships in cases of child abuse. This chapter focuses on some of the factors which influence how these formal systems operate in practice when members of the different professions concerned are required to work together on particular cases, for, as Tibbitt (1975, p. 14) argues: 'organisational arrangements in themselves are not a sufficient condition for successful integration if personal inter-relationships between the professions involved run counter to them.'

In certain respects interprofessional work in the field of child abuse is distinctive, for example, the feeling which parental violence to children engenders in the staff involved and society generally, the professional anxiety surrounding these cases and also the extent to which interprofessional communication has been formalised in the organisational arrangements made for handling the problem. But, interprofessional work in cases of child abuse can simply illustrate the fact that whenever individual workers collaborate, they bring both their own professional identity and their views about the role, status and frames of reference of other professions.

It is inevitable in a society characterised by division of labour, in which health, welfare, education and legal functions are provided by specialised occupations, that individual workers will spend a considerable amount of time in liaison with others in the interests of their patients, pupils or clients. Studies of social work activity, for example, show how large a proportion of social work time is spent on this process. One study of work in children's departments (Grey, 1969) showed that some 39 per cent of social work time was spent in face-to-face contact with clients while 23 per cent of time was spent in discussion with colleagues and with other agencies and a further 22 per cent on correspondence and case papers. More recently Goldberg *et al.* (1977) have shown that a high proportion of the referrals to social services departments concern practical and material problems, whose resolution often necessitates contact with other services and agencies. Our recent research into social service teams has shown social workers to be generally accepting of work of this kind, viewing it as an unavoidable consequence of work in a local authority department. Although Kane (1975), in a monograph on interprofessional teamwork in the USA, has demonstrated the central role of social work in much of the liaison and inter-agency work, it is by no means exclusively a social work activity but one in which all professionals have to engage. Yet such work—telephone calls, letter writing, attending meetings—is often described dismissively as administration and viewed as a tiresome distraction from the 'real' work of face-to-face contact with clients or patients. Clearly, some of the activities subsumed under the title 'administration' and currently carried out by professional staff could more properly and perhaps more efficiently be performed by administrative and clerical staff. Several of the committees of inquiry into cases of child abuse have revealed difficulties of communication within and between professions—notably in record-keeping and message-taking—caused, at least in part, by inadequate levels of clerical and administrative support. But it would seem inevitable that a certain and perhaps increasing amount of time will be spent by professionals in communication with each other if the complex and fragmented welfare services are to function effectively.

A study of social work education carried out as part of our research into social service teams revealed that out of a list of topics which might be covered on social work training courses, the two which were considered unimportant by the highest proportion of students were 'attending meetings' and 'committee behaviour'. Thus it seems that in practice and in training, relatively little attention is paid to the importance and the development of skills in interprofessional work.

Kane (1975) comments on how little systematic information is available on the subject of interprofessional work despite the current 'immense preoccupation with the nature of interprofessional practice' in many spheres of social service provision. Webb (1975, p. 6) makes a similar point concerning the British scene:

> Better co-ordination and teamwork are a perennial desire of planners, administrators, teachers and researchers in the social services. It is unfortunate that in Britain we have hardly begun to analyse what it is we are urging upon practitioners; why it is we are doing so; how much we think it is worth paying for better co-ordination, or how we might recognise good co-ordination— or teamwork—when we see it.

Furthermore, much that is written about interprofessional work

concerns interprofessional *teams*. Teams in this context vary widely
in their composition, cohesiveness, style of operation and the focus
of their work. Rubin *et al.* (1975) suggest that a team exists simply
when the job requires that people work together and co-ordinate
their activities. Teams are, however, usually characterised by a
greater continuity of inter-action than is generally the case with
interprofessional work on cases of child abuse in Britain. Some
centres here are providing services to abusing families on a teamwork model, such as the one at the Park Hospital in Oxford
(Ounsted *et al.*, 1975). Many individual workers function in intra-
professional teams in social services departments, or in interprofessional teams in primary health care settings or paediatric
units in hospitals. But most professional activity concerning child
abuse cannot properly be described as teamwork because of the
intermittent nature of the contact between the workers concerned,
some of whom may be only peripherally involved. The significance
is that there is therefore less opportunity to learn about and
accommodate different professional perspectives or at least agree
to differ, than there is when a team works together over time.
Goldberg and Neill (1972) describe this process in a multi-
professional team in general practice (p. 170): 'The creation of a
regular, well-organised channel of communication made it possible
to discuss problems in an orderly fashion, to forge a common
language and to clarify different approaches and perceptions as an
on-going process.' By contrast, in child abuse cases some, at least,
of the professionals attending case conferences may be meeting for
the first time, and very few are likely to be working together
regularly. In such circumstances, a greater reliance on stereotyped
views of the other professionals involved is to be expected.

   In two other respects, the understandings gained from studies of
interprofessional teamwork are of only limited usefulness in considering interprofessional work in child abuse. The first is that
much of the work examines only a part of the networks involved.
There are studies of links between schools and social services (for
example, Fitzherbert, 1977 and Robinson, 1978), between police
and social workers (Brown and Howes, 1975) and there are many
descriptions of joint work between health and social services which
have been summarised by Tibbitt (1975). In child abuse, however,
these and many others, such as housing and supplementary benefits
officials, may need to work together and there are few systematic
studies of these across the board relationships. Jefferys's (1965)
study of social welfare services in Buckinghamshire is perhaps the
most comprehensive, although, in some respects, now rather dated.
Secondly, many of the accounts of co-operation describe innovations

and experiments characterised by staff committed to the ventures, with a marked pioneering spirit. However, much interprofessional work is more mundane, taking place day by day between staff likely to range all the way from the committed to the antagonistic. Kane (1975, p. 21) has noted the paucity of 'research which indicates how different professions perceive themselves and each other and their expectations of each other in a working situation.' Two points emerge clearly from the studies of interprofessional work. First there is widespread ignorance about the training, role and perspectives of other professions and, linked with this, a lack of congruence between the self-perception of particular professionals and the way others perceive them. As a health visitor in the case conference study remarked of social workers: 'We do not understand what they do and they have no clue or idea what we do and this seems to be a basic problem.' The lack of congruence is illustrated by Kane (1975) who cites a study by Olsen and Olsen (1967) which found that physicians did not view tasks such as helping patients with their social and emotional problems or with adjustment to being in hospital as social work functions. Furthermore the physicians did not consider that social workers would view these as their functions, while the social workers believed that the physicians expected the social workers to carry out these tasks. As Kane (1975, p. 30) notes, 'with such confusion one wonders how a team process could function at all'.

It is not surprising then that stereotypes abound and there are many illustrations in our case conference study and the literature, for example: 'To the perceptive policeman whether in a panda car or at the police station the attitudes expressed and the actions taken or not taken by the (often young) social worker who has been sent to deal with the latest crisis may be seen as naive, too psychological or perhaps even totally inappropriate' (Kilby and Constable, 1975, p. 47). Social workers perceive health visitors to be 'poorly trained, insensitive to any but narrow physical factors and having doubtful judgement' (Dingwall, 1978, p. 25). While health visitors, on the other hand, 'present social workers as slow, as lacking in practical knowledge . . . ' (Dingwall, 1977, p. 150). In our case conference study a teacher finds 'that many of my colleagues are critical of social workers and there seems to be a sort of hierarchy here. The police are saying the teachers are too soft and I don't know who the social workers are saying is too soft.' And, a final example: 'Social workers are seen as do-gooders, social reformers and perpetual students whereas the police are seen as untrustworthy, intolerant of any deviant group and imposers of middle-class standards on the rest of the community' (Kilby and Constable, 1975, p. 49).

These are simply a few of the stereotypes affecting interprofessional work. One of their functions is to provide a framework—some order and predictability—within which relationships between professionals can be conducted. A second is to reinforce group solidarity. Another is that stereotypes enable professionals to distance themselves from each other and thereby to simplify issues. One of the present authors (Stevenson, 1973) has discussed the issue in relation to links between social workers and supplementary benefits officials, suggesting that social workers might have found the supplementary benefits commission a convenient scapegoat and that, consequently, they had an investment in not seeking to understand the commission's way of operation lest *'tout comprendre c'est tout pardonner.'*

One of the dictionary definitions of the word 'stereotype' is an 'unchanging conventionalised idea' and it is therefore to be expected that there will be some discrepancy between a stereotype and the 'real' world. Although technically a stereotype may be neutral, the quotations above illustrate that they are often used pejoratively and there are likely to be major problems in interprofessional work if the gap between the stereotype and the reality becomes too large. If, using one of the examples quoted above, health visitors are perceived by social workers to be 'insensitive to any but narrow physical factors', then they may well only listen to that part of a health visitor's observations which confirms their preconceived ideas—or prejudices—and minimise or ignore other information. It is a facet of only hearing what you want and are expecting, to hear.

Drake (1975, p. 87) considers the problem of stereotyping, linking it with labelling theory. With reference to a social services department, although her question can usefully be applied to individual staff, she asks:

As we are now aware, people live up to expectations of their behaviour; how far, therefore, do we rigidify a system and fossilise a department by unconsciously or consciously accepting someone else's definition of us, and to what extent do we also, as agencies, define ourselves in over-simplified stereotypes and then engage in a series of quite artificial encounters and movements with other bodies, which preclude real interaction?

Some of the work on interprofessional teams and liaison schemes (for example, between social workers and GPs or supplementary benefits officials) suggest that unhelpful stereotypes can be broken down through closer personal contact than normally occurs in everyday interprofessional communication. However, much depends on the nature of the contact, particularly if there is conflict. And it is, of course, possible that one's worst fears can be confirmed. It seems, therefore, that an important task for the helping professions is to seek to respond as openly as possible to other professionals in an effort to overcome stereotypes where these are damaging, and to examine more closely the occupational identity and frames of reference of others to clarify the nature of the differences between them.

It is important, however, to note that the occupational groupings are not monolithic and unchanging but contain distinctive subsystems with differing aims and values. Within the medical profession there are major differences in orientation between the specialisms, for example, between the high-technology cardiac surgeon and the 'whole person approach' of the psychiatrist or the general practitioner. Similarly, social work embraces practitioners with different types of training, including many with none, who practise in a variety of settings in the statutory and voluntary sectors and use interventive techniques ranging from community work to psychotherapy. Yet while recognising that within any profession there will be a good deal of diversity and deviance from group norms, it seems none the less that there is a more or less clearly defined identity which distinguishes one occupational group from another. Kahn (1974, p. 14) writes that 'general medicine, psychiatric nursing, social work and related disciplines remain convinced of their essential integrity, coherence and relevance' and 'there is no serious move to amalgamate, combine or join up'.

The way in which these identities are formed is complex. They result from certain social and personal characteristics which affect occupational choice (sex, class, personality, general educational attainment) inter-acting with training, occupational socialisation and role. It is difficult to disentangle the relative importance of these variables in the process of gaining an occupational identity. There are studies of professional training such as Becker *et al.* (1961), Davis (1975) and Dingwall (1977) which show its importance in affecting values and attitudes as well as in teaching knowledge and skills. McLeod and Meyer (1967) in an interesting paper describe an American study which compares the values held by trained social workers with those undergoing training and with untrained social workers. They suggest that 'selection and training operate to produce a professional group distinguishable in terms of certain value positions' (p. 414). But, while trained social workers were distinguishable from the less trained there was considerable variation among the trained social workers in their social values. In a subsequent article, Meyer *et al.* (1968), demonstrate that teachers as a group can be distinguished from social workers in respect of their values. Social workers, for example, place greater stress than do teachers on the importance of the worth and dignity of the individual as opposed to the supremacy of the goals of the group, state or social system. They also emphasise more than do teachers the responsibility of the group—whether family, community, or state—for individual welfare, while teachers place more emphasis on individual responsibility. Meyer *et al.* also studied the effects of occupational socialisation within the agency (as well as selective 'dropping out' from the profession) and show, first, that the longer teachers are in post the greater is the difference between their values and those of social workers and, secondly, that teachers with the same background characteristics hold different values in different types of school, thus producing substantial intra-occupational differences.

These studies illustrate some of the effects of training and agency socialisation in producing occupational identity. Such factors, however, build upon and inter-act with the background characteristics of the various professions thus producing a professional identity and an interprofessional status system. Two of the most important of these for interprofessional work are social class and sex, which reflect wider status differences in society. Social and educational mobility notwithstanding, there are substantial differences in the social class background of the professions. A survey carried out in 1966 for the Royal Commission on Medical Education (Cmnd 3569, 1968, p. 121) showed that the proportion of medical students drawn from 'the higher social classes' was 'substantial and increasing'. Banta and Fox (1972), in a study of role strains in an American health care team, found marked differences in social class between the social workers and the public health nurses and attribute to this some of the tension between the two groups. One of the nurses in that study commented: 'You know the social workers wear fantastic clothes out here. Every day. That sets up barriers. It couldn't help but make people aware of social and economic differences. To me this was another barrier, I couldn't imagine any communication taking place.' This well illustrates Kahn's point (1974) that, given the social class differences, efforts at communication have to be made across not only professional but also cultural space.

There are substantial differences in the sex composition of the different professions. Nursing remains a predominantly female occupation and although the proportion of men in social work has increased in recent years their distribution is unequal since more are in management positions than in basic grade posts. Simpson and Simpson (1969) argue that it is no coincidence that the semi-professions—the term used by Etzioni (1969) to describe nursing, teaching and social work—have a bureaucratic form of organisation and contain a higher proportion of women than the older professions. They suggest that this is a consequence *inter alia* of public unwillingness to grant occupational autonomy to women rather than to men, of women's stronger attachment to family as opposed to work roles and of women's acceptance of the general cultural norm that women should defer to men. This affects the relative status of different occupational groups and the working relationships between them—a point considered later in this chapter in relation to health visitors and doctors.

It may be possible at a high level of abstraction to define a common ethic and focus of work which unites the human service professions. Prins and Whyte (1972, p. 3), for example, cite as evidence of a trend towards unity between medicine and social work, the fact that both professions have in common 'a life dedicated to social service'. They draw attention to the increased emphasis in medical training on human development and human relations and suggest that 'any dichotomy between medical and social care is more apparent than real'. It seems more fruitful, however, not to seek a spurious unity but rather to recognise the differences in outlook and function between the professions and to agree with Kahn (1974) that in interprofessional work the aim is 'to "act together" and not to "think alike".' Some of these interprofessional differences are, therefore, examined below to illustrate the perspectives which may be held by five of the occupations which have crucial roles in relation to the problem of child abuse—health visiting, medicine, the police, teaching and social work.

HEALTH VISITORS

The first profession we consider is health visiting which shares with the other occupations discussed in this chapter some uncertainty about its role and function in a changing society. Yet health visiting seems to have particular problems in this respect. Uncertainty about the health visitor's role is not new. Jefferys (1965) in her examination of social welfare services in Buckinghamshire found that, when compared with workers in the other occupations studied, significantly more health visitors considered their job to lack a clear definition. The fieldwork was carried out in 1960-1 and health visitors made comments such as: 'Health visiting as a profession is missing the boat altogether and falling between all manner of stools. It would have been much better if most health visitors were still bedside nursing except for a minority who should become either social workers ... or specialists in health teaching' (p. 85); and: 'There's a lack of definition in the job. We're all things to all men. We're not regarded as social workers as such, yet we deal with all kinds of social problem' (p. 82). There is a striking similarity between these views and those of the Committee on Child Health Services (the Court Committee) which, more than fifteen years later (Cmnd 6684, 1976, p. 73) reported:

> Behind the assertion that too few GPs appreciate the independent responsibilities of the health visitor, we believe lies evidence that her special skills are too often being used for help of a kind more properly sought from social workers, and used increasingly for patients other than children and their families. However, it is also a reflection of some uncertainty about their role on the part of the health visiting profession.

Most health visitors are currently trained on a year's course which contains academic and fieldwork placements and follows their three-year training as state registered nurses and a midwifery training. (The precise effects on health visitor training of the government's decision to establish a unified central council for nursing, midwifery, and health visitors are, as yet, unclear.) It is the combination of these trainings, a total of some four years, which leads health visitors to describe themselves as 'highly qualified' (Jefferys, 1965, p. 84). The important point for debate, however, is how far the general nursing training is a relevant preparation for the health visitor's role. The Council for Education and Training of Health Visitors (CETHV), in a pamphlet on the function of the health visitor (1965), specify the knowledge brought to the health visiting service from the general nursing background to be human biology, principles of bacteriology, processes of disease and therapeutic methods. It may be argued that, as health visitors move increasingly into the 'social' side of their work, this 'medical' knowledge may become less relevant. It is also possible that experience in the hierarchical organisation of hospital nursing, with its emphasis on curative work and a 'submissive' pattern of work relationships with hospital doctors, is unhelpful preparation for the more independent, and, in theory at least, egalitarian model of teamwork in the primary health care team. Dingwall and McIntosh (1978) suggest that part of the health visiting training is devoted to 'unlearning' inappropriate models from the hospital nursing background and Dingwall (1977, p. 156) writes 'the extent to which health visitors are still nurses, given that they do nothing which is, commonsensically, nursing work, is an issue for many of them.'

Topics covered on the health visiting course include individual development through the life cycle and in relation to social and cultural groups, the development of social policy, social aspects of health and disease and the principles and practice of health visiting. These topics are, however, all covered in a one-year course. This suggests that to describe health visitors as highly qualified by formal training for the role which they are in fact required to perform may be somewhat misleading.

The formal definition of the health visitor's role offered by the CETHV (1965) stresses the prevention of mental, physical and emotional ill-health; the early detection of ill-health and the surveillance of high risk groups; the identification of need and the mobilisation of appropriate resources; health teaching and the provision of care through support, advice and guidance in cases of illness and in the care and management of children. Health visitors themselves point to the long-term preventive nature of their work with the general population, as well as their expertise in relation to medical problems and child development as factors which distinguish their task from social work (Dingwall, 1977).

What health visitors actually do is much affected by their membership of primary health care teams based in general practice. 80 per cent of health visitors now practise from GPs' surgeries. While retaining a responsibility to initiate contact with clients and a statutory duty to visit families with children under five, the focus of the health visitor's work has moved from widespread prevention to more selective intervention as they are asked by the GPs to deal with a wide variety of social problems arising in the practice. Dingwall (1977) has explored the tensions which arise between an emphasis in health visitor training on the role of the health visitor as an independent but equal member of the primary health care team and the reality of attachment with a pattern of subordination to medical dominance. As one health visitor in the case conference study said: 'We get a lot of referrals from doctors which are not, strictly speaking, health visiting referrals, though we have got to contain the situation somehow.' Thus, Bennett *et al.* (1972) note that when 'many general practitioners refer all social problems to their attached health visitors, irrespective of the medical component', then 'many health visitors from choice and in some cases out of necessity have come to accept a mixed health visitor/social worker role'.

The Court report (Cmnd 6684) states that work with children

under five is estimated to account for only 59 per cent of health visitors' time. The difficulty in balancing preventive work, particularly with children, with other demands arising from attachment to general practice was clearly illustrated in the evidence presented by the Health Visitors' Association to the Select Committee on Violence in the Family. They state that, in theory, 'health visitors really could play a large part in preventing the causes of family violence if there were enough of them to make regular visiting possible' (HC 329-II, 1977, p. 98). Yet they suggest that, in reality, health visitors are concentrating on people with identified social problems, including families at risk, and are taking on a more curative role.

This highlights a central ambiguity in the health visitor's role in that, although no longer a nurse, she is not a trained caseworker either. The recommended staffing level for the health visiting service is one per 4,600 population (or one to 3,000 in certain areas) but inquiries into cases of child abuse have revealed serious staff shortages. In the area with which the Auckland report was concerned, for example, there was one health visitor for every 10,000 people and in the area covered by the Steven Meurs report one to 11,000 population.

It is not only a matter of caseload size, however, which accounts for the relatively small number of health visitors appointed as key workers to work intensively in cases of child abuse, as found in our case conference study and by Castle (1976). A related difficulty, often stressed by health visitors, is their role as 'friendly visitor' with no statutory right of entry to private homes. (In fact, there is often misunderstanding amongst the professionals involved about the very limited circumstances in which the police and social workers are empowered to enter a private home.) The implications of their emphasis on 'friendly visiting' for the willingness of health visitors to give evidence in court are discussed in later chapters. With potentially very large caseloads which include not only child abuse cases but also a wide range of social problems, health visitors have to set limits on their intervention. And it is often at this point that difficulties with social workers arise. This is partly because, as part of the process of professionalisation, each group is struggling to define its functional specificity—that group of tasks which enables a profession to secure an identity different from its close collaborators and competitors. This is no less a problem for social work than it is currently for health visiting, although as Dingwall (1978, p. 21) argues 'to a considerable degree the rise of social work has been at the expense of health visiting', and access to many resources, such as day nursery places or aids for the physically handicapped, are now controlled by social services departments. At a time of pressure for both services, difficulties centre on the referral process between the two services. The problem for health visitors is that the social services' response to their referrals is too slow or is simply a refusal to take the case. Social services departments, or more usually team leaders who allocate in-coming work, have developed criteria, which may or may not be explicit, for accepting work. Thus, as a health visitor said in the case conference study:

> If we refer cases to the social services, they seem to have quite strict criteria for referrals, and there are some that they will take and others they won't; and we haven't yet developed criteria for refusals, with the consequence that when a real sort of crisis situation flares up, we're the people on the spot being pestered and we've got to do something. If we refer the situation, so often they are so busy that they don't deal with it for about a week, by which time most of the heat has simmered down and had to be dealt with by us.

Although health visitors generally pay less attention to 'routine' prevention than some would wish, it is clear that they none the less see many more 'normal' families in their work than do social workers with their current focus on dealing with people with problems in crisis. In 1974, for example, health visitors had some contact with 77 per cent of children under five (Cmnd 6684, p. 73). It is, therefore, not surprising that, at present, the definitions of 'acceptable' standards of child care or of 'urgent' cases should differ between the two professions. What is not clear, however, is whether, with less demand on their services, social workers would accept more readily a greater number of the referrals made by health visitors, or whether there is a fundamental difference of opinion between the two occupations as to what is considered appropriate for intervention by social workers.

At present, it is clear that structural problems in the health visiting role affect relationships between the two services and it is not, as was often stated in the case conference research, the personality of those involved which caused the widespread 'little local difficulty with the health visitor'. In the consultative document on priorities for health and personal social services, the DHSS proposed a 6 per cent increase in health visiting services, 'to allow for improvements in monitoring child health and welfare and support to mothers' (DHSS, 1976b). Yet if this is to be effective, attention will also need to be paid to clarification of the health visitor's role.

DOCTORS

Doctors in many of the medical specialties within the national health service have a role to play in the prevention, detection and management of child abuse. In primary health care there are the general practitioners, clinic medical officers and school health doctors. In hospitals there are the paediatricians and also psychiatrists, orthopaedic surgeons, neurosurgeons, obstetricians, radiologists, and staff in accident and emergency departments. In addition there are doctors with administrative duties, such as the community physicians with responsibility for child health, and those working outside the national health service, for example, in the prison medical service.

As was suggested earlier in this chapter, there are differences in orientation between doctors in these various forms of medical practice. The Auckland report (1975) illustrates how these differences can affect communication between doctors particularly when technical terms are used. The committee considered that the consultant psychiatrist to whom Mr Auckland had been referred by his GP did not inform the GP sufficiently clearly of the result of the consultation. The psychiatrist's own words in evidence, quoted in the report (p. 24), are as follows:

My report to [the GP] employs terms of clinical evaluation of the facts presented, the meaning of which are understood in full by me alone; which would be understood by a psychiatrist of similar experience to a considerable extent; but which would be less meaningful to a general medical practitioner, whilst providing him with a useful frame of reference.

There is little available information about the perspectives which the doctors in the various specialties generally bring to the problem of child abuse. Those who contribute to books and symposia under titles such as 'a view from the accident and emergency department' (Hall, 1975), 'A neurosurgeon's viewpoint' (Till, 1975) or 'An obstetrician's view' (Anderson, 1977) are usually distinguished from their colleagues in having a particular interest in the subject. Nevertheless, despite the differences within the profession, there are three features of medical practice which affect interprofessional work and which are widely shared by doctors, by virtue of their common occupational socialisation in training and subsequent employment.

The first concerns the frame of reference derived from medical knowledge. In common with training for other 'human service' occupations—teaching and the police, for example—medical education has recognised a need to take into account the findings of social science. The Royal Commission on Medical Education (Cmnd 3569, 1968) was critical of the lack of contribution from the behavioural sciences to the undergraduate curriculum and recommended that greater attention be paid to the social and cultural context of illness and doctor/patient relations. While the Royal Commission and wider social pressures have had some influence on medical education in this respect, it is difficult to assess how significant or how enthusiastically received, have been the contributions of the sociologists, social workers, social administrators, social medicine and public health staff and others mentioned in the report. Certainly the predominant focus of the curriculum remains biological and doctors are trained for the major part in high technology, specialised teaching hospitals.

The biological model with its emphasis on physical signs may lead some medical practitioners to conceptualise child abuse too tightly as a 'syndrome' which, as Richards (1975) suggests, is inappropriate given the variety of ways in which it occurs. This was illustrated in the case conference study by a general practitioner who did not agree that a child who had been injured by his parents was a case of child abuse because, when the parents were questioned in the accident and emergency department, they admitted that they had inflicted the injuries. Parental denial was a vital element in this GP's model of the 'syndrome'.

A second feature of medical practice is the extent of the personal responsibility carried by doctors, particularly in matters concerning clinical judgement. Dingwall (1978, p. 10), citing Atkinson's (1977) study, describes medical education as 'essentially a training for personal responsibility and a sense of self-confidence amounting to dogmatism'. In similar vein, Oppé (1975) writes: 'the doctor is trained to wield extraordinary individual power and responsibility.' Oppé suggests that the emphasis on exercising individual responsibility can make doctors reluctant or ineffective participants in case conferences, where many people may contribute to the decision-making and where, as is discussed in Chapter 3, the doctor may well not be 'in charge'. Certainly it is not surprising that there are some difficulties in co-operation between doctors and those professionals, such as social workers, who work in more tightly controlled bureaucracies with a need to refer certain decisions 'up the hierarchy'. The power of the GP or of the hospital consultant to take certain decisions and commit resources is undoubtedly greater than that of field social workers. A GP who gave evidence to the Select Committee on Violence in the Family illustrated the problem:

I have attended one case conference and I have made a private resolve that that will be the last. It was so time-consuming and, we feel, unproductive because it took away the decision-making from those who are responsible for making decisions and we were left with a decision to meet again and not take a decision pending the next meeting whereas those of us who were involved with the family had to get on and take some action (HC 329-II, 1977, p. 179).

A third feature of medical practice, which distinguishes it from some others with which it has to co-operate, is the pace of work. The doctor's work-style is generally characterised by decisiveness, directiveness and a shorter time-scale when compared, for example, with that of social workers. This may be due in part to the relatively greater certainty of medical knowledge and to the immediate nature of some, although by no means all, medical problems. Regensburg (1974, p. 51), reporting on an interprofessional workshop in America, writes that doctors described their work orientation as 'to do things rather than to solve problems' and she suggests that doctors often need and expect quick results. In this context it is of interest to note that the Royal College of General Practitioners estimate that the ordinary consultation in general practice lasts, on average, six minutes (HC 329-II, 1977, p. 153).

Two medical specialties, paediatrics and general practice, have a particularly important part to play in child abuse cases. Paediatricians in the USA and in this country have been in the forefront of developing knowledge and interest in child abuse. Indeed, some such as Helfer (1968), have argued that it is the responsibility of the medical profession to assume the leadership in this field. Pföhl (1977) has written that paediatricians were prepared to join with paediatric radiologists in promoting concern about child abuse. He suggests that this was a way of preventing the drift of paediatrics to 'professional marginality', following the reduction in life-threatening infectious diseases in childhood as a result of advances in preventive medicine and the use of antibiotics. This explanation for paediatricians' interest in the problem is related to the intra-professional status system in medicine which accords higher prestige to doctors who are in direct clinical practice and taking a high degree of risk, that is with responsibility for life and death situations (Becker *et al.*, 1961).

Child abuse now forms a significant proportion of the workload of hospital paediatric departments. One estimate is that, at any time, some 10 per cent of admissions to children's hospitals may be for proven or suspected non-accidental injuries (HC 329-II, 1977,

p. 109). In part, the volume of work stems from the emphasis placed on non-accidental injury as one manifestation of child abuse and consequently the crucial diagnostic role of paediatricians in assessing the significance of injuries, arranging for X-ray and haemotological examinations and so on. But government circulars and local procedural guidance have also recommended that children suspected to be at risk of injury be admitted to hospital under the care of the paediatrician to provide a 'place of safety' while the case is considered and decisions are made. Some of the criticisms of this policy are discussed in Chapter 1 but whether or not admission to hospital is always advisable, the contribution of paediatricians to the management of the problem remains important.

For paediatricians, work of this kind is undoubtedly time-consuming, involving a good deal of activity which is not strictly 'clinical', such as interviewing parents, attending case conferences, providing evidence for the juvenile courts. Those paediatricians who write on the subject are usually 'committed to the cause' and they often put forward a holistic view of their specialism stressing the importance of medical and social components. Thus Cooper (in Franklin, 1977a, p. 157) writes:

> Where psychological and family problems are particularly relevant to the child's condition the paediatrician will spend a good deal of time assessing the full psycho-social picture often with help from the social worker, health visitor, teacher, psychologist, or child psychologist. In no case is this more important than in the family problems of child abuse and neglect.

And Helfer (in Helfer and Kempe, 1968, p. 25) writes that the doctor

> with the assistance of his psychiatric and social service colleagues must make the diagnosis, protect the child, counsel the parents, report his findings and follow up, both medically and socially to assure that the proper disposition has not only been made but also carried out.

He continues with the important observation that 'many physicians are unwilling to accept this responsibility' and there are certainly indications that not all paediatricians share his commitment to this particular branch of the specialty with its large 'social' component. In our case conference study individual staff could contrast those consultant paediatricians in the locality who were interested with those who were not, and this was often reflected in attendance at case conferences. One junior doctor said in an interview following a case conference: 'I'd never have come into paediatrics if I'd known it was going to be like this.' Thus, in relation to inter-professional communication, these individual variations in perspectives must be taken into account.

While the child is in hospital, the consultant paediatrician is responsible for the immediate case management—a matter of clinical judgement—alongside the social services department's legal responsibilities for child protection and the provision of substitute care if required. In many cases there will be agreement between the various professions involved and, as Cooper (1977) notes, social work and paediatric expertise will often complement each other. Yet difficulties may arise when there is a difference of view, particularly between the paediatrician and the social services department, as to which course of action will best serve the interests of the child. Rapoport (1960, p. 118), describing a therapeutic community in a mental hospital in which 'treatment' was shared by all community members (patients, lay therapists, nurses, doctors and others), writes of the particular difficulties facing the doctors: 'In the doctor's role more than any others there is a marked discrepancy between the formal basis for authority and expectations with regard to responsibility on the one hand and the Unit's ideological tenets on the other.' Similar discrepancies between the doctor's formal authority on the one hand and the social services' responsibilities on the other arise in relation to child abuse. The extent to which doctors' opinions on issues within and outside medical matters are respected at case conferences is discussed in Chapter 3. Paediatricians have high professional status and are in a position of considerable power in relation to child abuse. Yet they are unable to initiate care proceedings (although their evidence is often vital) or to provide certain key resources such as day care places. Thus, although paediatricians can expect to have the final word in decisions on clinical matters, they cannot expect similar authority in relation to social care, for here they are in a dependency relationship with social workers.

By contrast to many paediatricians, GPs tend to play a less active role in relation to child abuse. Our case conference study confirms the well-known difficulties of securing the co-operation of some, although not all, GPs in multi-disciplinary work with cases of child abuse and in particular their poor record of attendance at conferences. Amongst GPs there is an interesting debate concerning their role in relation to child abuse and neglect, and individual GPs respond in different ways depending on their interests, attitudes and aptitudes. Some argue that the GP's role is simply to detect the problem if cases are presented to him, make appropriate referrals to the social services department and the hospital paediatrician, and share any relevant knowledge of the family at a case conference. Others see a more directive role stemming from the GP's duty 'to provide all necessary medical care and attention to children both for physical and emotional conditions' (HC 329-II, 1977, p. 152); this might involve offering counselling help to the parents and so on. What is not in doubt is that relevant information concerning the physical and mental health of the child and his parents, plus background knowledge of the family, is of potentially great significance in assessment and in formulating treatment plans for these cases. The GP, therefore, has a vital part to play, at least in the initial case conference.

One of the factors likely to affect GPs' perspectives on child abuse and neglect is its significance in relation to their total workload. Estimates of the incidence of abuse are notoriously unreliable, beset as they are by problems of definition and by concealed and unreported cases. It has been estimated that GPs might see on average one case every five years, but it seems that this figure may now be too low, given heightened awareness of the problem and sharper diagnostic skills. The Royal College of General Practitioners suggest that 'those general practitioners who are interested in this condition' report an incidence of one per thousand of the practice population (HC 329-II, 1977, p. 149). In one practice of some nine thousand patients twelve cases were recognised in a three-year period (Beswick, 1977). This forms a tiny proportion of the GP's workload, which, in turn, has important consequences. In general they are bound to be less experienced and less confident than when dealing with other more routine aspects of their work. They are also likely to be less knowledgeable partly because until recently the topic was not covered specifically in their basic medical education, but also because GPs are widely reported to be 'poor attenders' at locally organised in-service training days on the topic.

We discuss in Chapter 4 the intense feelings which may be aroused in professionals by parental violence and their resistances to recognising the problem. This may be a particular problem for those GPs who have a long association with families in the practice, possibly spanning the generations. Aside from any worries about confidentiality (also discussed in Chapter 4), this may be one of many powerful reasons for taking no action, particularly if the patient is perceived to be the parent rather than the child. Another reason for a reluctance to take action may be that of losing direct control of the situation as the child abuse procedures, and many other people, are brought into the case following notification to the appropriate agency. A related difficulty, if the GP makes a referral, is that the law may be brought into operation in respect either of care proceedings in the juvenile court or, less frequently, criminal prosecution of the parents. General practitioners share with others, notably health visitors but also social workers, a reluctance to give evidence in legal proceedings while having to continue to work with the family.

These constraints on action may help to explain why studies of sources of referral of child abuse cases indicate that GPs come low down the lists. One study (Skinner and Castle, 1969) showed that the referral rate from GPs was 3.9 per cent, and another (Castle and Kerr, 1972) that it was 2.9 per cent. The findings of Castle and Kerr are particularly interesting since in 60 of the 292 cases studied (nearly 20 per cent) children were treated for the referred injuries by their GPs only. It may be that some cases of abuse identified by GPs are referred to the appropriate agencies by the health visitor attached to the practice. However, as Castle and Kerr write, whether GPs are slow to identify cases of child abuse or slow to refer them is, in the present state of knowledge, a matter for speculation. Stone (1977) and Beswick (1977) make clear that there are many GPs with an interest in the problem who are willing to play a full part in helping these children and their families. But there is also evidence that some GPs are, for a variety of reasons, unwilling to participate in the procedures for diagnosis and management of child abuse recommended by the DHSS and by local area review committees. Thus their knowledge of many families and their potentially key role in early detection of the problem are not used to their full potential.

THE POLICE

One of the sharpest differences in professional perspectives may be seen in respect of the police role in cases of child abuse for as Carter (1977, p. 202) has argued, 'child abuse is or is not a crime according to the ideology of the onlooker.' The difficulties arise principally in disagreements about the appropriate place of the criminal law in relation to child abuse rather than over police involvement in obtaining place of safety orders. Two statutes govern the operation of the criminal law in respect of injury to children. Section 1 of the Children and Young Persons Act 1933, under which most criminal proceedings concerning child abuse are brought, provides that it shall be an offence for any person over 16 having the custody charge or care of a child or young person to assault, ill-treat, neglect, abandon or expose him in a manner likely to cause unnecessary suffering or injury to health. The other relevant statute is the Offences Against the Person Act 1861, which deals with cases of assault. An assault is defined as: 'the intentional application of force to the person of another without his consent or the threat of such force by an act or gesture if the person threatening has or causes the person threatened to believe that he has the present ability to effect his purpose' (HC 329-II, 1977, p. 30). It can be seen that this definition of the word 'assault', 'the application of force... without consent', differs from its common usage in that there is no connotation of seriousness or gravity of the blows inflicted. Technically, any slap or blow is an assault. The rights of parents to chastise their children are, however, recognised at common law and provided the chastisement is moderate it is a good defence in a charge of assault on a child to prove that the circumstances amounted to lawful correction. None the less, under these two statutes, assault and ill-treatment and neglect of children are crimes and some difficult issues concerning the police role in family violence stem from this in view of the responsibility of the police to prevent and detect crime.

Some of the difficulty surrounding police intervention in cases of child abuse may reflect wider uncertainty about their role in a changing and pluralist society. In police training there is now increased emphasis on the social aspects and context of their work and their basic training covers the handling of domestic disputes, with lectures on subjects such as assault, children, urban problems. However, as is well illustrated in relation to juvenile crime, there is some tension between 'hard' and 'soft' policing, that is, between detection and prosecution on the one hand and prevention and rehabilitation on the other. In consequence, as Dear (1975) suggests, the police find it difficult to define their role adequately or to determine what is required or expected of them.

Anxiety concerning the police role in relation to child abuse centres on two issues: in what circumstances, if at all, should they investigate suspected cases and when, if at all, should they prosecute. Both issues are linked with police attendance at case conferences. It seems that for other professionals involved, the role of the police may create difficulty not so much over their decisions to prosecute in the comparatively infrequent serious cases, but over their involvement in routine investigations of suspected abuse.

The police view concerning investigation as revealed, for example, by Collie (1975), Mounsey (1975) and Wedlake (1977), is that where child abuse is suspected, the duty of the police is to investigate the circumstances. They emphasise that the police have the facilities, the training, the skills and the experience in carrying out inquiries to arrive at the 'truth' about what happened. They stress the importance of receiving early notification so that the police can interview those concerned before the trail is cold and other explanations of events have been devised. They argue that this not only protects children but also protects parents against unsubstantiated allegations and grave suspicions. The police view in this matter was unequivocally expressed by the Association of Chief Officers of Police in their evidence to the Select Committee on Violence in the Family as follows:

> Every case must be regarded with a degree of suspicion, and it is incumbent upon the social services, medical profession, hospitals, etc. to ensure that the police *are* involved in a case at the earliest possible stage. The police service *must* [their emphasis] be involved in all cases of violence. The service carries the responsibility for the protection of life, and the prevention, investigation and prosecution of crime (HC 329-II, 1977, p. 32).

It is the stress on early notification to the police which may cause the greatest difficulty, for it implies that others involved, doctors and social workers, for example, should pass on information about *all* suspected cases without some preliminary sifting to decide whether police investigation would be appropriate. It is unlikely that in practice the police can be, and it may be inappropriate that they should be, 'first on the scene' for so long as injured children are taken to the accident and emergency department or the GP's surgery, or cases are reported directly to the social services departments or the NSPCC. The duties of all these practitioners to protect the child will involve an early interview with the parents, the child if appropriate, and other relevant people to assess whether the child's immediate removal from home is required.

The police desire to 'get in quickly' accounts for the recommendation in their evidence to the Select Committee that case conferences on all suspected or known cases of non-accidental injury should be convened within twenty-four to thirty-six hours of the case becoming known. This is a contentious suggestion for, particularly where a child's safety has been temporarily protected by removal from the home, whether or not on a place of safety order, it might be better to hold the case conference after a few days than within the time span suggested by the police. This would enable a more systematic collection and collation of previous knowledge of the family from a variety of sources, which can be a time-consuming process, and it might facilitate better decision making by those concerned, when calmer mood prevails. On a more practical point, it is likely that many of those whose presence would be required—doctors, teachers, social workers—would be unable to attend at such short notice, particularly since these cases form, as they do with the police, only a proportion of their workload.

It is not, however, simply practical difficulties about timing which affect notification to the police, for many professionals would argue that police investigation, however skilful, is inappropriate for many of the known or suspected cases of child abuse coming to their notice. This view is held particularly when the injuries to the child are slight, although there may still be a good deal of concern about the child's welfare. The argument is that these families are often subject to multiple environmental and personal stresses; are in need of 'help' not 'punishment', and that 'help' is the best way of protecting the child and his interests. In particular, they would question the emphasis placed by the police on finding out the 'truth' about the injury inflicted. For, the argument continues, the injury is only one of the 'truths', and may not be the most important about the family and its functioning, all of which are relevant to the protection of the children. This is not to suggest that observing and taking a detailed account of the injury and of the explanations offered and trying to establish what happened is unimportant. (In the past many doctors, social workers and others have paid insufficient attention to this and this is criticised in the reports of several committees of inquiry into child abuse, for example, in the Colwell report and the Lisa Godfrey report [1975, p. 8]). It is to suggest, however, that the events surrounding the 'injury' need to be placed within an understanding of the family relationships that is as full as possible, and that 'hard to reach' parents may not find it easy to disclose this type of information during or following police investigation. The need is for a full social and physical assessment of the child, parents and their family functioning rather than only for a criminal investigation into 'an injury'.

This view is not unanimously held, however, by some of the professionals involved who argue that police investigation is a positive, even therapeutic, action which faces the abusing parent openly with the reality and gravity of his actions and can thus prepare the way usefully for future help, usually social work intervention. Some also suggest that the presence of 'the law', in the form of a visit by a police officer, may be a powerful deterrent to further abusive behaviour, but it seems likely that this would depend on the particular circumstances of each case. It may, for example, prove effective in restraining over-chastisement in fundamentally healthy families in which injury to children is not habitual, but it is difficult to see it as appropriate or helpful in some of the very disturbed patterns of parenting associated with some cases. Thus a decision to request selective visiting by the police to achieve these purposes in particular cases would seem to be more effective than reporting all cases for routine investigation.

This raises an issue about which there seems to be some confusion—namely, whether there is a duty incumbent on workers to report all cases of child abuse as suspected 'crimes' to the police. Goodman (1975) writes that there is generally no enforceable legal duty of giving information to the police, although it is an offence (under the Criminal Law Act 1967) to accept 'a consideration' for failing to disclose information which might help in securing a prosecution. Thus any duty to report suspected crime is moral, in aiding law enforcement, rather than legal, provided the professionals involved had not been paid to keep quiet.

The primary purpose of police investigation is to enable a decision to be reached as to whether the parent (or care-taker) should be prosecuted. As in other criminal matters, the police can and do exercise discretion about whether or not to prosecute, and the decision is the responsibility of the chief officer of police, in consultation, if necessary, with the Director of Public Prosecutions. Police views about the circumstances in which prosecution is appropriate, even when there is evidence to support a criminal charge, seem to vary. Wedlake (1977) and Collie (1975) stress that prosecutions by no means always follow investigations in child abuse cases, but Mounsey (1975) writes that while the police appreciate the social and environmental factors associated with abuse, the protection of the child must be paramount and therefore, he argues, 'in some if not most cases this must inevitably lead to prosecution of the offender.' The police stress that prosecution is not necessarily harmful to rehabilitation and that the court, after finding the facts, will be concerned with the help and support to be offered to the offender. Thus, child abuse cases well illustrate the wider debate concerning the balance and tension between justice and welfare, between punishment, retribution and rehabilitation in the penal system.

Further study of the effects of prosecution in cases of child abuse, on the parent or parents prosecuted, on the injured child and other siblings, and perhaps on the parent who is 'left behind' if only one is prosecuted, is required. In its absence the temptation is for us all to harbour prejudices. It may be argued that prosecution is unlikely to deter parents with poor impulse control who may have been harshly punished in their own childhood. In these circumstances prosecution is likely to reinforce their low self-esteem.

Tibbits (1977), on the other hand, suggests that some parents may want and seek the protection of the law to prevent them from doing wrong. The police stress that they take account of the individual family circumstances and the advice of other professionals in reaching their decisions about prosecution, but they are understandably anxious that others should not decide to exempt this category of offenders from the investigative process and the criminal law.

It is not surprising that these different perspectives as to whether or not child abuse should be treated as a crime have centred on the police role in attending case conferences. While practice varies from authority to authority and many instances of good liaison appear to exist, as in our case conference research, the subject was of sufficient concern for the DHSS and Home Office to issue a letter of guidance in 1976 (DHSS and Home Office, 1976). This stressed that the police, in common with other agencies, retain the capacity to take action independently of the case conference in certain circumstances. None the less, the departments considered that area review committees should work towards police attendance at all case conferences concerning non-accidental injury to children. The letter puts considerable emphasis on the police supplying to case conferences details, where relevant, of the criminal records of members of households under discussion and making available the valuable information they may have derived from previous dealings with the family. As in the Colwell case, these may often be derived from domestic disputes or investigating allegations that children have been left alone.

The 'low key' tone of the guidance in relation to the police role in prosecution and investigation of cases of child abuse is particularly interesting. For example, it says (p. 3):

> In considering the need for an investigation, the Departments hope that where a case conference has been held chief officers of police (whilst retaining the capacity to take independent action) will take into account any views expressed by the conference about the effect of an investigation on the welfare of the child.

This suggests very clearly that the duty of the police to investigate the circumstances of cases of assault is not absolute, and that they have discretion not simply about whether to prosecute but also about whether to investigate.

In practice it seems that the problems can be and often are resolved by notifying the police of, and inviting them to, all case conferences concerning non-accidental injury to children, with the expectation that they would postpone any investigation until after the conference. With regard to prosecution it seems that there is a consensus amongst many of those involved that it is appropriate in those cases involving very serious injury or death, for the protection of the law cannot be denied to children in these circumstances, nor can such a serious breach of the law be tolerated.

TEACHERS

In common with other professions considered in this chapter there is considerable diversity within teaching, between the primary and secondary sectors, and amongst individual teachers in their orientation. Indeed, Evans (1977, p. 97) writes: 'I am tempted to say that one of the difficulties of education is that there is not a professional stance. There are 440,000 teachers, no general teachers' council, there are twelve professional associations ... ' This diversity, in itself, makes it difficult to discern a common perspective and the problem is compounded by the teachers' relatively low profile on child abuse and neglect. There are several indications of this. It is interesting to note that, while the Ministry of Defence submitted evidence (in respect of non-accidental injury to children of service families) to the Select Committee on Violence in the Family, the Department of Education and Science did not do so, nor did the teachers' professional associations. Similarly, the Tunbridge Wells Study Group, an important multi-disciplinary advisory group on the subject of child abuse, had members drawn from nursing, medicine, law, the police and social work but not from teaching. A third example comes from the DHSS letter of guidance (1974) which, in making recommendations as to the composition of case conferences, states that they should normally include 'persons having statutory responsibilities' for the continuing care of the child, such as social workers and the consultant in charge of the patient's medical care, and 'persons concerned with the provision of services likely to be relevant to the case', like the family doctor and health visitor. Teachers, however, are listed under the heading 'others who may also be invited when appropriate'.

A major reason for the lack of attention to the teachers' role in child abuse has been the emphasis, or, perhaps, over-emphasis, paid to non-accidental *injury* as one manifestation of the problem. It is clear that non-accidental *injuries* are more commonly inflicted (or detected) on children under school-age than on older children. The study of cases reported to the NSPCC special unit registers in 1975 (Creighton and Owtram, 1977) reports 69.9 per cent of the cases as involving injuries inflicted on children under 5. Furthermore, their findings also confirm that younger children receive more serious injuries than children over school age who are likely to be more resilient or able to avoid the blows. None the less, 21.4 per cent of children receiving injuries described as 'moderate' were aged between 5 and 10 years. As the concept of child abuse widens to include emotional abuse and, more recently (Kempe and Kempe, 1978) sexual abuse, the likelihood of older children being involved increases. It is also the case, given the length of time which abusing families may remain in treatment, that some at least of the children injured in early childhood will still be the subject of professional concern when the child, and his siblings, are of school age. Thus it seems that the teachers' potential role in relation to child abuse is unlikely to diminish in the near future, and it may well increase.

Child abuse is, however, only a small aspect of the teachers' work for their primary purpose is to educate children within the school system. As Robinson (1978, p. 203) notes, 'teachers, while paying attention to the world of the child outside the school situation, must focus on the educational tasks of the school.' But she adds, 'the crucial dilemmas centre on the definition of the educational tasks.' Within teaching, there is considerable variation in how widely or narrowly these 'educational tasks' are defined and in the place of the welfare function within schools. Fitzherbert (1977) illustrates something of the diversity. At one extreme are head teachers 'who adhere to the philosophy that the teacher's responsibility for his pupils ends at the school gates and at the end of the school day' (p. 139) while at the other extreme are head teachers who attempt to shoulder responsibility for all welfare matters arising in the school. Of these Fitzherbert writes (p. 140): 'an overdeveloped sense of responsibility for the welfare of children in a head teacher can be of limited effectiveness unless it is coupled with the ability to share his load with others, outside professionals as well as fellow teachers.' These quotations illustrate how important is the head teacher's view of the welfare function in the school, for this can set the pattern for class teachers in such matters as whether they can communicate directly with other professionals, such as social workers, whether they have face to face contact with the educational welfare officer or whether all contacts are with the head teacher, and whether class teachers can attend case conferences. The importance of these internal arrangements was well illustrated in the Maria Colwell inquiry and they are discussed at some length in the report (1974).

The personal and professional values of teachers are important determinants of their orientation to the welfare of children in the school. One study which compared teachers' values with social workers' and found significant differences between them (Meyer *et al.*, 1968) was cited earlier in this chapter. A similar but small scale study in England (Craft and Craft, 1971) produced rather different results, finding teachers and social workers not unfamiliar with the content of each other's role and a high degree of consensus between the two groups on factors such as the importance of home background information in teaching and on the importance of social factors in the educational process. Part at least, of the differences in findings between these two studies may be attributed to the fact that the population studied in Craft and Craft's work was a self-selected group attending a course on the inter-relationships of home, school and welfare.

Hart (1978), however, confirms the finding of a good deal of consensus between the stated aims and values of the teaching profession compared with social work. Hart suggests that the most significant differences between the professions are to be found in their methods of operation which are more easily visible than aims and values. Teachers work almost exclusively in groups and employ more directive techniques and this has consequences for the attention which can be paid to any one individual's needs within the group's goals. Kahn (1974, p. 16) writes of this:

> The value system of the school, for example, requires that a child be considered a competent, functioning learner. If he cannot perform, he may be supported by a limited number of program adjustments and environmental manipulations. Those who help him must reaffirm the validity of the school's institutional mission and the assumption about his basic capacity. Anything beyond this changes the school as an institution to a point where it is dysfunctional for the learning of the majority. What, in fact, if the child cannot function under such circumstances because he lacks the personal capacity; what if the manipulations which can be accommodated by the school as an institution are not enough? Then, I believe, 'outside' help is needed, whether in a child guidance clinic, a day program, or a residential treatment center. In short, it is the case that a given institution has its outer limits of elasticity and one must recognize this in deciding when to seek help elsewhere.

The crucial question is where the outer limits of elasticity are perceived to be. But, wherever they are, it is indisputable that teachers are well-placed by virtue of their close daily contact with pupils and often with their parents or the local community 'grapevine' to get to know about children and their families who are causing concern in the context of child abuse and neglect. (Such opportunities are also available to those providing day care to the pre-school child in day nurseries and play groups.) Some teachers with particular interests in the welfare function may use this knowledge to make early referrals to the appropriate agencies, whether to educational welfare officers, the school health service, educational psychologists or to outside agencies. Other teachers, who may not have initiated referral, are likely to prove a vital source of information about the school-age child at risk of abuse. The detailed and perceptive observations of class teachers seen in our case conference study are discussed in Chapter 3 and the Maria Colwell case well illustrated the potential importance of the teacher's contribution.

SOCIAL WORKERS

This chapter ends with a discussion of the role of social workers in relation to child abuse and neglect—an area where local authority social workers have a central part to play on account of their statutory responsibilities for child protection. Uncertainty about the nature of social work, which exists both within the profession and amongst those with whom they collaborate, poses a major difficulty for social workers in interprofessional work. There are several strands to the uncertainty. One is simply that the term 'social work' is broader and more vague than some others, such as teaching or policing, and its meaning is not immediately clear to those unfamiliar with it. While health care and education are universally provided and very widely used, social work is provided much more selectively. Thus, many of those involved in interprofessional work have no personal experience of social work to underpin their understanding of social workers' roles and functions. (We should perhaps note, however, that personal experience of the professional service of others may not always facilitate interprofessional work. Teachers, in particular, point out the dangers of others thinking they 'know all about it' and making generalisations about education from their personal experience of school, often some years ago. As Evans, 1977, p. 101, notes, 'confident ignorance masquerading as knowledge is highly dangerous.') While studies of the transactions between social workers and clients (Mayer and Timms, 1970 and Lishman, 1978) and between doctors and patients (Boyle, 1975) reveal gaps in the understanding of the process between the 'helpers' and the 'helped', it seems that there is a clearer general understanding of the purposes and methods of medicine than of social work.

Another strand in the uncertainty about the nature of social work is its relative newness as an occupation and in particular the recent and rapid development and expansion of services. In the thirty years following the creation of children's departments in 1948, the range of tasks and responsibilities undertaken has increased greatly and new responsibilities continue to be added by legislation, such as the Chronically Sick and Disabled Persons Act 1970 and the Children Act 1975. The creation of social services departments may, as the Seebohm committee envisaged, in itself have stimulated demand for services. But this is difficult to establish because while there was undoubtedly an increase in demand in the early seventies, this may have been related to certain other factors. First, the Chronically Sick and Disabled Persons Act placed upon local authority social services departments for the first time a duty to seek out the needs of the disabled. This had extensive implications in terms both of resources and the organisation of service. Secondly, a period of high inflation brought many people to social services departments simply because they were in financial difficulties, especially over fuel bills. Thirdly, the predictable growth in the numbers of the frail elderly produced ever increasing requests for domiciliary service, especially for home helps.

As recommended by the Seebohm committee, social workers were appointed to direct social services departments. (There were a few, strongly contested exceptions.) Yet social work, as such, represents only a small part of the work of a social services department. Whether or not one accepts that social work should properly be at the centre of these organisations, it seems likely that the rapid growth of the 'service component' in social services departments has held back the clarification of the task of the social worker, which had been hotly debated in earlier years. Hospital social workers in particular had struggled to dissociate themselves from a service-oriented view of social work. Once national health service and social security provision freed them of their 'almoning' responsibilities, they were able to make some headway in convincing the other professionals with whom they worked, notably doctors, that they were not primarily 'service providers'. As the debate concerning the nature of the social work task continues, the current emphasis on practical service may tend to confirm other professionals in beliefs about social work that social workers themselves once sought to refute.

If the growth of social services departments has contributed to confusion about the task of the social worker in them, none the less, in organisational terms, social services have 'come a long way fast' in establishing a base distinct from medical influence and consuming a high proportion of local authority expenditure. The typical pattern of organisation within the large departments is to decentralise fieldwork and domiciliary services (and at times residential services) to area teams which serve a discrete part of the authority's patch, comprising some or all of the following staff: area management staff, social workers, social work assistants, home help organisers, occupational therapists. Incoming work is usually dealt with by the duty officer (a function which social workers perform in rotation) or by a team of specialist 'intake' workers. As with schools, these organisational arrangements within social services departments have important repercussions for interprofessional collaboration. A GP or teacher with patients or pupils drawn from a wide catchment area may have to relate to several different decentralised teams often with different work priorities, rarely made explicit to other agencies, depending on the staff level, pressure of work and balance of interests within the team. Furthermore, each time contact is made with a particular team, the referral is likely to be dealt with by one of a number of changing duty officers, leading to the complaint, often made by doctors, that 'you never get the same person twice'. In addition, with generic practice the number of social workers who could, in theory, deal with any particular client group has increased although in practice there is much informal specialisation.

Also consequent upon the creation of social services departments, the power relationships in interprofessional work have changed with the transfer from the former local authority health departments of some resources, such as home helps or day care. Social workers, therefore, now act in a crucial role as gatekeepers to the considerable resources controlled by social services departments, whether of residential, day care, or domiciliary services or of social workers' time. In cases of child abuse and neglect they largely determine access to care proceedings.

Alongside the rapid development in the organisational context of social work, and affected by them, there has been a continuing debate within social work, with contributions from outsiders (for example, Wootton, 1959 and 1978) about the nature and purpose, methods and efficacy of social work. This is part of the process of establishing an occupational identity distinct from other helping professionals, for example, psychologists, psychiatrists, and some nurses whose knowledge base, skills and function may overlap, at least in part, with those of social workers. There are, however, other significant elements underlying the debate. One is that social workers, in adopting a model of practice derived at least in part from dynamic psychology, were subjected to the same question as psycho-therapists and psycho-analysts—'How do we know it works?'. The growth of empirical research in the social sciences enabled this question to be asked with greater rigour and precision (although not always with sufficient subtlety, given the nature of the interactions which were being investigated). 'Caseworkers' came under scrutiny and sometimes attack. Various empirical studies (for example, Reid and Shyne, 1969, Davies, 1969 and Goldberg, 1970) have shown how hard it is to establish the efficacy of such intervention, although, to be fair, the tools of study are as yet crude and not all the findings as pessimistic as some have implied. However, other modes of intervention, with radically different underlying assumptions, have not fared much better. For example, evaluative studies of community work, such as that of Halsey (1972), have been similarly inconclusive.

Thus, the rise of social work as significant in terms of resources and power *vis-à-vis* other professions has been accompanied by professional self-doubt and soul searching, in which not only efficacy but goals have been questioned, in a climate which is at one scientifically more sophisticated and ideologically more contentious.

Another approach in the search for a social work identity has been particularly important, namely, the attempt to define the 'generic' in social work. To many other professionals, and also to many British social workers, the word 'generic' has been used to mean work 'across' client groups. However, this is not the sense in which it has been generally used in the literature, especially that from the USA, which has sought to find a framework to encompass practice and theory across different methods of intervention and different practice settings. This concern is reflected in the content and titles of such books as Bartlett (1970) *The Common Base of Social Work Practice*, Pincus and Minahan (1973) *Social Work Practice: Model and Method* and Goldstein (1973) *Social Work Practice: A Unitary Approach*.

The search in this country for a social work identity is still in progress, reflected in the BASW report *The Social Work Task* (1977) and in Butrym's (1976) work, and this causes difficulty for social workers in giving a clear and concise explanation of their function to other professionals. A second difficulty in establishing interprofessional relations is the lack of homogeneity in type of training and function subsumed by the term 'social worker'. At times the title is applied simply to those occupying social work posts whether professionally qualified or not, but there is also considerable diversity within social work training.

Social workers can take courses of varying lengths, related to their previous educational and occupational experience. The Central Council for Education and Training in Social Work (CCETSW) has recently reaffirmed its policy of recruiting approximately half graduates and half non-graduates to the courses recognised for the award of the Certificate of Qualification in Social Work (CQSW). Some years ago, most graduate social workers were considerably younger than non-graduate ones, so that this policy had clear implications for the age structure of the profession. Whilst this is still generally true, there has been a recent trend towards younger students in the non-graduate entry. None the less, those who communicate with basic grade social workers may find themselves talking, at one extreme, to a 24-year-old honours graduate in history with two years' professional education or, at the other, a 40-year-old with little or no formal educational qualification but more than twenty years' work experience in perhaps industry and youth work, followed by two years' professional education. It is not, therefore, surprising that other professionals may at times feel uncertain in face to face inter-actions. In child abuse cases, however, there is a greater likelihood that the social workers involved will be qualified since this work is accorded the highest priority within social services departments and usually allocated, wherever possible, to qualified and experienced staff. However, the distribution of qualified staff varies greatly throughout the country and the BASW report on registers (1978) produced following a survey of practice in some seventy-seven local authorities, found that in 85 per cent of them unqualified social workers were, at times, working with families in which child abuse had occurred.

An important question in interprofessional work is the extent to which, through training, agency socialisation and the legislative framework within which they operate, social workers share certain values likely to affect the way they approach their task. As with each of the professional groups examined in this chapter, there is considerable diversity within social work. The debate about values, inextricably linked as it is to objectives, has been lively and at times acrimonious. The CCETSW, identifying the issue as crucial in social work education, set up a working party whose report *Values in Social Work* (1976) indicates the struggle which the group had in reaching the degree of consensus necessary to publish anything at all. The report, *inter alia*, considers the implications of certain religious or ideological commitments, such as Christianity, Zen Buddhism and Marxism. It also discusses certain 'stances', such as 'the liberal view' or 'the mechanistic view' of human nature, and the impact of Freudian and Existentialist theories upon social work.

From this and from a study of the standard texts, used by generations of social work students, several crucial problems emerge. The first is that when fundamental values are expressed at a high level of abstraction, such as 'respect for persons' or 'the client's right to self-determination', it becomes difficult, if not impossible to claim these as distinguishing social work from other helping professions. To do so is misleading and pretentious. Yet it is the way in which these values are expressed in practice which may highlight points of difference between professions. The CCETSW report (1976, p. 52) provides an example of this in comparing lawyers and social workers. The former would claim respect for persons as a fundamental value of their profession. 'Lawyers . . . are often irritated by the lack of precision in social workers' reports which fail to distinguish between observation and inference. They consider accuracy to be important in upholding the value of respect for persons.' Yet, as the report discusses, there are other aspects of legal attitudes and process which the social worker may believe are inimical to the 'respect for persons' value.

We cannot consider these matters in the depth and detail which they deserve and the above serves only to illustrate what is a complex and highly significant element in professional interaction, namely, the way in which value systems are interpreted in practice and in which certain scientific, ideological, or religious perspectives on human beings both create and affect value positions.

A further point concerns the relationship between ethical standards and treatment models. Most social work students have been taught that to impose their wishes on clients is not simply unethical but unlikely to succeed. The problems which come to social workers are many and various and it would be foolish to deny the usefulness and acceptability of straightforward advice on many occasions. It may be that social workers have been over-cautious about this in the past and that this has been a cause of interprofessional friction. (They have also been justly accused of ignoring the influence and power implicit in the structure of the relationship.) But in the matters with which we are here concerned, most social workers would hold that social work help to abusing parents is more likely to succeed if the parents are given every opportunity to express their feelings about the children and their situation, so that treatment plans are built upon a shared understanding of the stresses which caused or contributed to the problem. This affects the pace of work, a point of interprofessional conflict to which reference has been made earlier.

However, perhaps the most important area of value conflict between social workers and other professionals concerns the deceptively simple question—'Who is my client?' There are two elements in this.

The first, rather elusive aspect of this question relates to the social worker's role in the protection of society as well as of the client. Although this may, on occasion, arise for other professionals, notably psychiatrists, it is perhaps more pervasive in the daily activities of social workers. Younghusband (1978, Vol. 2, pp. 142-3) has analysed this well.

> In many situations, social workers were caught in conflicts about balancing their responsibilities to the client, their employer and their professional integrity...Social workers gave an uncomplicated allegiance to the principle of self-determination in the period when they were trying to discover why people acted as they did and to help them to make their own choices rather than to force moralistic solutions upon them. The principle became less clear-cut when attention shifted to the family, the group and the local community...The concept of participation, which came into the limelight in the 1960s was an aspect of self-determination under a more fashionable name. For some social workers this included the acceptance of each person as uniquely himself and of his right to be different but not to behave in ways which injured others.

The social worker's role as an agent of social control is often prominent in cases of child abuse and neglect, for she/he is called upon to intervene in the balance between the rights and responsibilities of family members when the behaviour of some may be harmful to others.

The second aspect of the question asks 'Is my client the family or the individual?' Beer (1975, p. 76) has noted the difficulty of coping with the conflict caused by reconciling the need for the protection of the child with the need to 'care' for parents. Social workers are at times accused of paying too much attention to the family, particularly the parents, and too little to the needs of children. There is some evidence for this in, for example, the Lisa Godfrey and Karen Spencer reports.

Our case conference research did not, however, reveal wide differences in the focus of concern on the part of the various workers involved. Davies, a health visitor, has written (1975, p. 81), 'workers are not in competition with each other but have the same goal of a happy child in a loving family.' Few would dispute such a statement and social workers are now enjoined by law, following the Children Act 1975, to honour the welfare principle in relation to children facing adoption or those in care. This states that those making decisions shall 'have regard to all the circumstances, first consideration being given to the need to safeguard and promote the welfare of the child throughout his childhood; and to ascertain as far as practicable the wishes and feelings of the child and give due consideration to them having regard to his age and understanding.'[1] The crucial question then is *how* to promote the child's welfare and it seems that such interprofessional disagreement as there is may be about means rather than ends. As Chapter 3 on decision making in case conferences shows, social workers bear the prime responsibility for making these decisions and they have to balance interests which are at times in conflict and make predictions on the basis of uncertain knowledge. Cooper, a paediatrician, has written (1977, p. 27):

> the mistaken notion that separating a child from his family is always a last resort and harmful is widely believed by social workers. In fact the contrary is true. Whatever the age of the child, removal from traumatic physical and emotional battering is always beneficial if the substitute care provides adequately for the child's needs.

The extent to which substitute care meets these needs is the crux of the matter. Stroud (1975, p. 96) indicates the complexity of the issue and sums up the social worker's dilemma well:

> The task of those concerned with child care is to attempt to assess how the welfare of the child can best be secured, given that much of the evidence collected, if not contradictory, will pull in different directions. Strengths in the family situation may be revealed as well as risks; in most parents, perhaps more often in mothers, there will be a detectable emotional ambivalence; or, while the family circle may be fragile, there may be a known lack of viable and satisfying alternatives in the shape of adoptive or foster parents. Even where such resources exist, the experience of the Children's Departments in the 50s indicates that there are risks in severing a child from his roots.

It is generally accepted that children need love and security, as well as new experiences, praise and recognition and responsibility, for their full physical, emotional, intellectual and social development (Kellmer-Pringle, 1975). It is also generally accepted, although some disagree, that these needs are most readily—they are certainly customarily—provided within the nuclear family. As Rowe (1977a, p. 147) writes:

> When a child comes into care, the aspects of family life which are most difficult to reproduce for him are commitment, individualisation, continuity, perspective and reciprocity in relationships. All these are regularly provided by even inadequate families. They are essential ingredients with which the child can build a sense of personal identity, a capacity to take responsibility for himself and for others and an ability to form lasting and affectionate relationships.

In a useful review of the outcome of foster and adoptive care Rowe concludes (1977a, p. 154) that although adoption carries 'its own inherent hazards as well as its proportions of outright failures', nevertheless for children needing permanent care 'the adoption picture is considerably more encouraging than the fostering one'. The dilemma for those making decisions in each case of child abuse is to balance the somewhat uncertain knowledge about outcomes in substitute care with predictions about how the child might fare in his own family, and to relate these assessments to the child's needs. As one of the present authors noted in the Colwell report (1974, p. 109), 'the harsh lesson which social workers in the child care service have had to learn is that, so far as children in long-term care are concerned, there are very few situations in which choices are clear-cut and outcomes predictable.' Such considerations would, in any case, lead to a situation in which the decision to separate a child from his family was not taken lightly but this is reinforced by the legislative framework in child care which, while shifting the balance between children's and parents' rights towards the former in the Children Act 1975, nevertheless demands that certain clearly defined conditions are met before children can be removed from their parents. Our case conference study revealed a good deal of uncertainty among the other professionals involved, about the legal framework within which social workers operate, and particularly about the grounds for seeking a care order under the Children and Young Persons Act, 1969.

It seems then that interprofessional differences in this matter stem not so much from social workers' over-reliance on 'the blood tie' but from their awareness of the difficulties of providing adequate long-term substitute care. This is not to suggest that there is no substance in the criticisms made of social workers for failure to plan decisively for the needs of children (see, for example, Rowe

and Lambert, 1973 and Goldstein *et al.*, 1973) which the Children
Act 1975 takes steps to remedy. In the field of child abuse and
neglect there are undoubtedly some parents so unable to offer an
adequate level of care that permanent removal of their children
must be sought. But these are a minority of cases. In the majority
the decisions are much less clear-cut.

Finally, one other difference in social workers' perspective on the
problem may be the extent of their fear of publicity in the event of a
tragedy. Social services departments bear the prime responsibility
for the protection of children. They have a statutory duty to
investigate any complaint that a child is being ill-treated[2] as well as
to provide social work or social services to prevent family break-
down and to provide care for deprived or neglected children. Thus,
in the published inquiries into cases of child abuse, the social
workers have been in central positions and public attention and
criticism has focused on them. This is of interest since several of the
inquiry reports reveal substantial failures in other services, notably
in education and the health services as, for example, in the Colwell
and Auckland reports. Yet these have usually passed with little
public comment apart perhaps from the role of the health visiting
service in the Steven Meurs (1975) report. We comment elsewhere
in the book on the effects of this anxiety but it seems relevant in the
context of interprofessional work to note the current vulnerability
of social workers, in particular, to public censure in these matters.

NOTES

1 Section 3 and Section 59 of the Children Act 1975.
2 Children and Young Persons Act 1969, Section 2(i).

Chapter 3

Case Conferences – their Background and Purposes

This chapter is about case conferences, which have come to assume a central place in the procedures for the investigation and management of cases of child abuse. We shall draw in part upon our research, carried out in 1976, a broad outline of which is described below. The intention is to use this study as a springboard for wider ranging discussion; obviously, some of the important issues concerning interprofessional communication are not unique to case conferences and in Chapter 2 the question of professionals' attitudes towards themselves and others is considered more fully. But such conferences often highlight the problems with particular clarity. In addition, the fact that such communication takes place within a group with a particular purpose and special characteristics raises some questions, which are different from those raised by an informal meeting of two or three people to discuss a case.

The case conference is not a new phenomenon. It has long had a place in the context of multi-disciplinary teams—a planned occasion when people required to co-operate in the care of individuals and families came together formally to discuss diagnosis and treatment. Reference has already been made to Kane's work (1975), which surveys the extensive literature on interprofessional teamwork in the USA. Given the complexities and uncertainties which Kane describes concerning interprofessional communication within the context of the team, it is salutory to remind ourselves of the high, perhaps unrealistic, expectations which have arisen in relation to such communication in child abuse, especially in relation to case conferences. The practitioner may be forgiven for some irritation with the exhortatory tone of much of the official literature on this theme. That the task in interprofessional communication deserves more study and less well-intentioned advice is well illustrated by the continuing problems in this area revealed by the most recent official inquiries into the deaths of such children as Simon Peacock (1978) and Karen Spencer (1978) four years after the Maria Colwell inquiry (1974), which dwelt at considerable length on this issue.

The history of the case conference in the UK in the past fifty years highlights some points of importance in the way it is presently used. Linked to teamwork as in the USA, it was most often found in settings concerned with the physical or mental health of adults or children. It was most firmly established in child guidance clinics. Members of the clinical team met to share information and to reach an agreed diagnosis and treatment plan. They formed the core of conference participants with outsiders (such as child care officers, after 1948) invited for a particular contribution. In the child guidance clinic the supremacy of the psychiatrist as the 'team leader' and chairperson of the conference was rarely, if ever, questioned; indeed, this is still usually the case.

The advent of children's departments in the UK in 1948 brought the conference into a new arena, in which medical leadership was no longer taken for granted. Many children's departments held case conferences at children's reception homes, to which psychiatrists and psychologists might be invited, but which were held under the auspices of the children's departments and usually chaired by a senior officer of that department. Thus the creation of an organisation for child welfare, separate from the medical services, altered the balance of power and perhaps, therefore, the emphasis in relation to the plans made for children in care.

Soon after the creation of the children's department the need for co-ordination of social services generally was recognised and is embodied in the 1950 circular referred to in the first chapter. This led to an extension of the case conference function to a meeting of all the relevant professionals and officials involved in the welfare of a particular family. Policies with regard to the convening and chairing of these conferences varied greatly from one authority to another; in particular, some authorities used medical officers of health as co-ordinators in chief whilst others placed these duties upon children's officers. The typical case conference of this kind was described and discussed by one of the present authors in 'Co-ordination Reviewed' (Stevenson, 1963). In it, an attempt was made to show how the definitions of role affected the perceptions of the family under discussion, a matter which is still highly relevant to our present considerations. What was not explored was the power structure of such meetings and how they affected decisions.

From the late 1950s the small but very influential development of therapeutic communities in mental hospitals also brought the case conference (often including the patient) into the forefront of treatment planning. Here again, medical supremacy, hitherto unchallenged, was called in question, albeit ambiguously. Such conferences were supposed to provide a democratic forum for the analysis of the problem and there was often no explicit statement as to where the leadership lay. None the less, there was usually an implicit assumption that the psychiatrist was 'primus inter pares'. This ambiguity was noted and criticised by Rapoport (1960), amongst others, and Kane (1975) has also drawn attention to it in relation to role blurring within teams.

Thus it can be seen that the case conference as an instrument for diagnosis and treatment has a long history and that, from a situation in which the medical purposes were paramount and medical authority was clearcut, we have moved in the last twenty-five years to one in which the medical/social components are increasingly recognised as inter-related, even inseparable, and in which it is no longer self-evident that doctors should control the conduct of the discussions which take place.

Against this background, some of the continuing uncertainties in the field of child abuse about the interaction of medical and social welfare personnel are better understood. Today's case conferences are in many ways a logical extension of those advocated in the 1950 circular. However, when the issue of physical injury is under discussion the relevance of the medical contribution to the diagnosis may be crucial, to a greater extent than in the more general discussion of the so-called problem families, who were often the subject of the earlier conferences. When they are held in hospital and the child in hospital is the subject, it is natural that the established authoritative role of the doctor is often to the fore. The authors observed two such conferences held in hospital, at which there was actual doubt as to whether the chair was being taken by the doctor or by social services. At another the chair was assumed by the doctor, to the irritation of the social worker who considered that it would have been more appropriate for her to do so. Apart from the specific question as to who should chair a conference, these inter-actions illustrate a complex issue of divided responsibility which has been discussed earlier—that although a consultant usually does not carry the ultimate responsibility for long-term case management he does have 'a duty of care' to his patient which may at times bring him into conflict with workers in social service departments. A conference held in a hospital where a child is being cared for is particularly likely to reveal such problems. In any case, some other professionals, including social workers themselves, will lean heavily upon the opinion and advice of the doctor, even in matters not medical. As one of our medical respondents put it: 'Once the doctor is there, the ball is put in his court and a lot of it is referred to him . . . whether or not he is the most suitable person.'

The inter-action of medical and social welfare participants at conferences must, then, be understood in a historical context concerning the balance of power, which has been affected by structural and organisational changes, and by the increasing recognition of the relevance of knowledge from the social and behavioural sciences to diagnosis and treatment. It is perhaps not surprising that this relationship is still often ambiguous and tense.

There are other professions involved in child abuse case conferences whose inter-action deserves further consideration and some aspects of this will be discussed later in the context of our research. However, given the history of interprofessional conferences, this particular facet of communication must be given special weight.

With growing awareness of the concern about child abuse, the use of case conferences as a mechanism for improving interprofessional communication was widely accepted. References to case conferences are contained, inter alia, in DHSS letters of April 1974 (DHSS, 1974) and of February 1976 (DHSS, 1976a). In their procedural guidelines a number of area review committees have been more specific as to when conferences should be convened than were the government circulars. For example, the 1976 letter appends the Durham area review committee guidelines, which stress the role of the case conference in 'retaining overall concern for the management of the case' and suggests that they should be 'reconvened at each significant development or when any professional worker is particularly worried'. Clearly this gives a very wide remit to the case conference, with room for differences of opinion as to when 'overall case management' and 'significant development' require the calling of a case conference.

Another procedural handbook[1] is much more specific; for example, it states that:

> It is emphasised that a case conference will be held at the earliest possible moment when a child is abused, believed to be abused or there are any serious doubts about the possibility, or if a child known to be at risk moves into the borough. The term abuse includes substantial and continuing emotional stress. The conference shall take place without delay and no conference shall be delayed because the full membership cannot be convened. All those who are involved, potentially involved, or who have relevant information, shall attend as a matter of course.

The prescriptive verbs like 'will be held', 'shall take place', leave no doubt that the area review committee is directing its professional staff how to act. In this sense, there is little room for discretion and

failure to convene an initial conference in the manner laid down
would lead to criticism in the event of a tragedy. None the less,
however hard those who frame such instructions strive to be
unambiguous, there is always residual discretion as to the interpretation of the phrases used, for example, 'without delay', 'substantial and continuing emotional abuse' and 'those who are . . .
potentially involved or who have relevant information'.

Such illustrations go to the heart of the problem of balance
between procedural accountability and professional independence
discussed in Chapter 1. There are some situations in which there
may be no room for argument after the event as to whether the
conference should have been called; for example, the same guidelines state: 'the case conference shall be recalled by the key worker
before a major decision has to be made, e.g. whether a child shall
be allowed to return home'. However, not all area review committees are as prescriptive. Rochdale area review committee's guidelines appended to the DHSS circular (1976a) concerning case conferences simply state: 'on receipt of the referral and following any
appropriate investigation it *may be thought necessary* to hold a case
conference' (authors' italics).

The Wayne Brewer inquiry (1977) highlights the issue well. The
committee's terms of reference required it to 'review the guidelines
which the committee have designed for those professionally concerned' (p. 1) but they decided 'not to undertake a detailed
examination of the present guidance given' (p. 6). However, they
devote a section of their report to the question of case conferences
and conclude that 'further consideration should be given to identifying more clearly the occasions when case conferences should be
convened when the child is already subject to a care or supervision
order and is either about to return or is already at home' (p. 46).

Their comment arises from the analysis of the Wayne Brewer
case itself, in which the committee notes four occasions when a
conference might have been called and was not and criticises the
social services department for not doing so in two of the four
instances. In fairness, they point out that the local guidelines were
not in force until February 1976, until the last phase of the case;
besides, it does not seem that the directives regarding case conferences were particularly specific in this locality. Thus, in this
particular instance, the committee did not criticise the workers
concerned for failure to follow definite procedures. Rather, they
concentrated on the professional judgement of those who might
have called a case conference and did not. That is to say, they were
concerned with responsibility, not accountability. It is interesting
that in neither of the two instances in which the committee thought

a case conference would have been helpful is it suggested that the professionals were not communicating effectively by other means. In the first, the committee comments (p. 28):

> There were frequent discussions between the professional workers about what should be done for his safety but no formal case conference was convened. We do not think that this resulted in any factors being left out of consideration but we feel that the formulation of a plan of management as a standard practice would have been helpful to those concerned, especially outside the social services department.

Of the second, they say (p. 29):

> We feel that the two incidents (of injury) put together, coupled with a pattern of mounting stress would have warranted the convening of a case conference which might well have helped to crystallise a plan of action to be taken.

Thus the suggestion is that the holding of a case conference might have firmed up the plans for action. The committee puts the case for such conferences persuasively (p. 30):

> We see as the advantages of case conferences the pooling of information relevant to the care and safety of the child. The total information yielded is likely to be a great deal more than the sum of the individual parts. Many professionals are inclined—erroneously—to assume they know what another's contribution will be. An opportunity exists for each participant to offer his interpretation of particular aspects of the situation and to contribute to the decision finally reached. Not only is each participant directly aware of the decision but because it is collectively arrived at he will have a fuller understanding of it and a greater sense of commitment towards its implementation.

This sounds sensible and is indeed in accord with the current received wisdom, reflected in central government circulars and area review committee guidelines up and down the land. Yet, whilst not wishing to challenge the basic assumption of the usefulness of conferences, it is perhaps wise to view them with a degree of healthy scepticism. There is no magic in holding a case conference; its effectiveness depends in large measure on the presence and knowledge of key people and on the quality of the chairing. Furthermore, as will be discussed later, it does not go without saying (or proving) that the quality of decisions reached in such groups is inevitably better than those taken by one or more persons in less formal circumstances. Certainly, it is to be hoped that, even when the guidelines are fairly specific, the mere fact that a conference was called or was not called will not weigh too heavily with those who, later, may be involved in inquiries when things go wrong. This is not to say that there cannot be a presumption that a conference would usually be desirable at certain crucial points (as, for example, when a care or supervision order may be revoked). It is simply to suggest that mechanical operational procedures can never be a substitute for professional judgement.

Thus far, we have considered something of the aetiology of the case conference within our social and health care framework and its significance in the context of child abuse. We turn now to describe and discuss the research into case conferences concerned with children at risk which the present authors carried out in 1976. This study took place in areas covered by three neighbouring area review committees in England. The findings are based upon attendance at thirteen case conferences and interviews with forty-nine, 87 per cent, of those who attended six of these conferences. We observed (but took no part in) the thirteen conferences, noting such matters as the conference composition, the role of the chairperson, the communication and inter-action between participants, including areas of agreement and disagreement, the jargon used, the main foci of discussion and the decisions reached. Our interviews with respondents were loosely structured. Topics included: the participants' background and experience of dealing with cases of child abuse and of attending case conferences; the nature of their contact, if any, with members of the family under discussion; their area of expertise and their understanding of the roles of others at the conference; their view of the purpose of the conference and whether it was achieved and an assessment of its effectiveness. We used participants' and researchers' shared experience of the conferences which both had attended as the basis for a broader consideration of case conferences in general.

Our study was concerned with the purposes and the processes of the conferences, the latter laying special emphasis on the role of the chairperson. This chapter discusses their purposes, how they may be defined and are translated into practice.

A recent working party of the British Paediatric Association and the BASW cited in Jones, McClean and Vobe (1978) has identified eight tasks for the conference. They suggest that these are:

(1) To share knowledge of and concern about the family,

including parental biographies and a full family history;
(2)	To formulate a diagnosis and full family assessment, including degree of risk in relation to the register of criteria;
(3)	To decide whether or not to recommend registration;
(4)	To formulate immediate treatment plan and long-term aims;
(5)	To allocate responsibility for the implementation of the plans;
(6)	To nominate a key worker;
(7)	To decide whether to inform the parents (and child if appropriate) of the fact and significance of registration, and if so, how and when this is to be done;
(8)	To decide an on-going procedure.

Our research headings, formulated before the working party reported, suggested that there were four broad purposes.

(1)	To pool information about the children thought to be at risk and their family circumstances, in order to build up as full a picture as possible.
(2)	To reach decisions as to action. There are many which are part of a general treatment plan (such as securing a playgroup place). The most serious in terms of consequences are: placing on the 'at risk register'; deciding on the prime worker; instituting legal proceedings to remove the child or children; and deciding to take no action.
(3)	To pool evidence about abuse which could be used in legal proceedings—a different process from information sharing;
(4)	To share, and sometimes to defuse, the anxiety which is inevitably felt by those most responsible and accountable.

The working party headings can readily be subsumed under our first three headings. Yet it is valuable that the working party in item seven drew attention to parental involvement. It is perhaps significant that at none of the conferences which we attended, or in interviews with respondents afterwards, was the specific issue of informing parents about the at risk register raised. (Nor was the issue of parents attending conferences raised spontaneously by respondents, although we asked their views on this point. However, there were several occasions when the conference participants discussed what parents should be told about the conference itself.)

In formulating conference purposes the present authors added a fourth, that of sharing, and sometimes defusing, anxiety. We believe it to be appropriate to accept this as an explicit purpose, alongside others which are focused on the problems and needs of the family. In work so stressful, we should acknowledge the support functions of the conference for the workers.

The primary, explicit purpose of the conferences we studied varied considerably. Of the thirteen, five were called to consider the need for removal of children from home on a place of safety or care order; three were to decide whether to place children on the at risk register, to appoint a key worker, and other related issues; three were to review progress of children already on the register and to plan future action, removal of the child from home being not currently under consideration. One conference was to review progress and to consider removing the child's name from the register. There was one in which the purpose was unclear.

This highlights the difference in degrees of urgency and levels of anxiety at different conferences, which is bound to affect the dynamics of the group. These are further affected by the kind of risk which is being considered. Although at all the conferences, some or all of the children had been defined as being at risk in general terms (not necessarily in need of registration) the meanings of the phrase were many and various and in some of the conferences there was disagreement as to what constituted risk. In eight of the thirteen cases, there was clear cut physical injury assessed to have been caused non-accidentally. In two, there was emotional risk and in one case there was 'moral danger'. Although in cases of physical risk, there was often worry about neglect or poor standards of care, in none of the thirteen was neglect the sole cause of concern.[2] It is likely that the probability of physical risk will create a greater sense of urgency than other less tangible risks. It is also likely that participants will react to different kinds of risk with different degrees of anxiety, which reflect their own value system and personal characteristics. This may be especially evident when neglect or moral danger are under debate. The definitions of the level of concern about such issues will vary. Participants are, therefore, likely to come to the conference with different mental sets about the problem under debate. Thus we can see that not only may conferences have more than one purpose but that their purposes may be differently perceived or emphasised by those who attend.

SHARING INFORMATION

Other points of interest and difficulty also arise from a consideration of conference purposes. One of these concerns the sharing of information. Some aspects of this are discussed later in relation to the processes of communication but the content is also of interest. Presumably the intention is to gather observations and information so as to gain a picture of family dynamics which somehow 'hangs together'. If it does not, that in itself may be noted as indicative of missing clues or an ambiguous situation. Whilst some of the conferences we attended left us with a relatively clear impression of the total family situation, others did not. We accept that those with extensive prior knowledge were much better placed than we to grasp the situation but at most conferences there were some present who, like ourselves, did not have such knowledge. These areas of doubt fell broadly under six headings.

The first concerns past and present social, medical and psychiatric information about the parents. Obviously the availability of this information depends to a large extent on who attends the conference. One key person here is the GP. Our study confirmed the observation made by others, referred to by several committees of inquiry and by government, that GPs rarely attend conferences. (They were present at three of the thirteen in our sample.) The absence of GPs from so many of the conferences in our study was clearly not unusual. Many of those interviewed mentioned it as a problem with views ranging from, 'The family doctor has never been to case conferences I've been to. They are a law unto themselves', to suggestions that 'they don't want to know. They are nervous about meetings.' Only one person interviewed thought that things were improving.

Some of the factors which may affect the attendance of GPs at case conferences have been discussed in Chapter 2. There are also practical considerations concerning the length and timing of the conferences, for example, that they frequently clash with morning surgery.

Whatever the cause, the absence of GPs from many of the conferences frequently left vital information gaps about the physical and mental health of parents and of the children themselves which could not be or were not filled by the health visitors attending on their behalf. It was not clear whether this was because health visitors were not in possession of the relevant medical information (and the brevity of medical records and the increasing use of locums on emergency service may be relevant considerations here) or because the health visitors felt constrained in the interests of medical confidentiality from disclosing medical information in the GP's absence. One nursing officer spoke of the difficulty for health visitors in standing in for GPs in this way:

This very often happens. The GPs expect us to stand in for them even if it's only on an informal basis, they will never actually say it but we will talk over the family beforehand. But it doesn't work that way. You can't go to a case conference and say 'Well, my GP said this' because that's hearsay and he's not there to say it himself. You can say, 'I've talked this over with my GP and he agrees with me' but that's as far as it goes.

This quotation illustrates some of the problems arising when the communications are planned informally yet the case conference is, in fact, a formal gathering. It certainly seemed that it was only of limited usefulness to the conference for health visitors and others to come 'bearing messages' since it was difficult for them to take discussions on from there.

However, GPs are not the only source of information about parental histories and the present situation. It is now less generally accepted that taking a social history is an integral part of good social work practice. The impact of 'labelling theory' on social workers and the concern it raises about processes of stigmatisation is part of the explanation. But the matter is more complicated than that. Taking a social history implies a theoretical frame of reference. The questions asked are related to a construct of social reality which selects and rejects certain information as relevant. Social histories in the past were usually linked to a psycho-dynamic interpretation of behaviour which has been widely criticised. But no coherent alternative has been substituted which would enable social workers confidently to obtain information. Yet in relation to child abuse some such information seems highly relevant. For example, there is some evidence that parents who abuse their children have often themselves been abused (although not necessarily physically ill-treated) in childhood. Such facts may of course have been known to those present at earlier conferences. But, if so, they were not much referred to or linked to present problems in the conferences we attended. In one case, for example, we learnt that the mother had a history of severe mental illness but few further details were forthcoming. By contrast, in another conference, there was a helpful description of the mother's severe childhood illness and maternal over-protection which put the present situation into context, although, again, we did not learn much detail of her hospitalisation and the nature of her illness. (There is a further problem as to how such information is understood and used by others present. We discuss this in Chapter 4.)

Whatever arguments there may be concerning the relevance of the past, there can surely be no dispute about the need to have up to date information about parents' present health, mental or physical and about their material and social circumstances. There were several conferences at which such information was missing. In one we learnt that the father (the assaulter) was physically disabled, but no medical or social details were forthcoming to fill out this information. (In fairness, this was a particularly difficult family to reach and it was not clear whether the father had ever consulted the doctor. He certainly would not let the social workers over the threshhold. But no one was able to clarify the nature and effects of his disability and its relation to the present problem.)

A second area of difficulty in achieving the conference purpose of gathering information concerns the danger of focusing too sharply on the risk to one child whilst neglecting others. The conferences we attended varied in this respect. In the majority, all the children were discussed. For example, at one where a decision was made to remove illegitimate twins on a place of safety order, careful thought was given to the possible repercussions on the other two legitimate children. However, of the eight families with more than one child, we felt there was some cause for concern that in three of them, all the children had not been, as it were, cleared or related to the child at risk. In one case, attention was focused, because of a relatively minor health problem, on the child possibly least at risk. Two of our respondents, who attended many conferences, said that 'very often the other children were completely overlooked'.

In this connection, a theoretical issue not discussed at the case conferences which we attended concerns the possibility of scapegoating mechanisms within the family and whether such processes might relate to one child only or be 'transferable' once that child was removed. Theories of family inter-action leave us uncertain about the factors which may place one child at risk where others are safe, although the research, for example by Lynch (1976), concerning difficult births and subsequent separation of mothers and babies may provide clues as to the likely special factors operating to make a particular child a scapegoat. It is interesting to note Bell and Vogel's (1960) comments, in a paper published nearly twenty years ago, which discusses 'scapegoated' children in families in a way which is clearly relevant to the present concern with the dynamics of families of abused children. They suggest that 'the selection of a child is not a random matter: one child is the best symbol' and that 'who is selected as the scapegoat is intimately related to the sources of tension' (p. 386). They continue, with reference to a sample of such children (p. 388):

> In a number of cases, the disturbed child either had a serious physical disease when he was young or a striking physical abnormality such as a hare lip . . . The mere existence of such abnormality

seemed to draw attention to one particular child, so that if there were some sorts of anxieties or problems . . . the child with the physical peculiarities seemed to become the focus . . .

We were interested in the connections between the child at risk of physical abuse and his general state of physical health and others in the family. There are three points here: first, one might expect a poor level of care to give rise to health problems; secondly, ill health in parents or children leads to increased stress and possibly periods of separation through hospitalisation; yet, thirdly, there were also some examples of cases in which some hereditary or congenital condition in the child might aggravate parental aggression to produce a scapegoating syndrome. Thus, in one case, the son of a PT instructor was thought to have some slight brain abnormality causing some oddity in behaviour and poor muscular co-ordination. The details were not, however, clear at the conference. In another case, however, a 3-year-old boy was found to be mentally retarded and physically ill co-ordinated so that there was at least a possibility that the somewhat improbable explanations of accidents were correct and that he might have been an unusually difficult child to control. In such cases the availability of up-to-date medical information at conferences, understandable to laymen, may be of great importance and the relationship of a child's physical health to parental attitudes and management should always be explored.

For accurate information, the presence of those who are in a position to observe the children closely in their daily activities may also be crucial. As mentioned in the previous chapter, the presence at the conference of such people as class teachers, nurses, playgroup leaders or residential social work staff may be an invaluable source of direct observation. Their attendance at the conferences we studied was patchy, in particular the class teachers were missed. Although few participants spontaneously raised this point, we were struck by the teachers' absence. Many of those interviewed seemed to accept the practice whereby head teachers normally represented schools at conferences and did not, therefore, suggest class teachers when asked about who else should have attended the conference. A few participants, however, suggested that head and class teachers jointly attended more often than was the case in our study. A class teacher was present in her own right at only one of the conferences and her contribution was vitally important in its concrete and detailed observations.

The head teachers interviewed explained, on practical and theoretical grounds, the practice whereby they and not class teachers attended. The practical problem was simply that: 'if the class teacher who's involved with the child goes I have to take over as class teacher'. Also, with families with two or three children in the school, or with team teaching, several teachers might be involved. The head teachers argued that theirs was the responsibility for the welfare of children in school. One said: 'I decided it's my job to go. For instance, I talk to the education welfare officer. She doesn't talk very often to other staff. It's likely I've been in contact with other agencies and I see it as my job to be involved in this way.' Another argued: 'this is not a monopoly of power and influence by heads. It's often the only way to ensure continuity. The school may make a commitment and the only person who should be in a position to make that commitment and have the overall view is the head.' This is not to suggest that head teachers attended conferences without knowledge of the children under discussion. They said they had specifically sought the views of the class teachers concerned before the conference, in addition to the on-going involvement they had with children experiencing difficulties in school. However, as with GPs, there is considerable value in those with first hand knowledge of the family meeting face-to-face with others to share information and take the discussion on to the point at which decisions can be reached. Castle (1976, p. 10) writes: 'Concern has frequently been expressed that key personnel are often represented by another member of their department who may have no personal knowledge of the family involved and consequently cannot be effective in the decision-making . . . ' Certainly, the evidence at the Colwell inquiry illustrated the point with particular force. Having traced the distressing failures of communication within and between the schools which Maria attended, the committee commented (1974, p. 67):

> It was strongly argued by the Chief Education Officer for Brighton that the responsibility for the welfare of individual children and therefore this contact with outside agencies, must rest with the head or his deputy . . . It is obvious that the ultimate responsibility must rest with the head master. The only question at issue is whether this responsibility may on occasions be delegated to the class teacher . . . what seems to us essential is that the class teacher is always involved; preferably through direct contact with the social worker concerned. We were impressed by this sincerity and perceptiveness of Maria which all three of her class teachers showed. We feel it is possible that anxieties about Maria's situation might have been conveyed with greater accuracy and urgency if her last class teacher therefore had herself spoken to [the social worker] in the Autumn term . . . [before she died].

How might the observations of those who are unable to attend conferences be given more weight at them? For if its purpose is to be achieved, there must surely be some solution to this dilemma. If time is the key problem, they might be invited to attend for a small part of the conference and to present their own direct observations and assessment. Another possibility for incorporating the views of those unable to attend is for someone closely involved with the case, perhaps the prime worker, to discuss it with them before the conference. In the case of teachers, the head teacher could not be expected to do this as effectively as the prime worker since the former would lack the detailed knowledge required. A third way would be for those unable to attend to submit their written views. It may be necessary to resort to these expedients. Yet they must be regarded as second best. For whilst we recognise that considerable discussion about the cases takes place outside the conference, the value of actually participating in the conference was illustrated in our study. We were struck as we observed the conferences by the way in which small, apparently trivial pieces of information assume a significance and coherence when put together with others to form a picture of the family and its problems.

Another point of importance in the completeness of the picture obtained at the conference concerns the fathers or step-fathers in the families. There was a marked contrast between the conferences in the amount known about fathers and, not surprisingly there-fore, in the help being offered to them. It was interesting that in the two cases in which there had been considerable effort devoted to direct work with the fathers (thought to be the parent responsible for the assault) there had been special workers involved. In one case an army welfare officer had played a prominent part; in the other, a probation voluntary associate had concentrated his attention upon the father. This is not to say that in other cases there had not been work with both parents and there were others where fathers were missing or unwilling to be seen. However, despite difficulties that there may be in reaching fathers in these cases, it is of concern that there were at least three cases in our study where the attitudes of the father to the problem seemed to be virtually unknown or were filtered through the mother, although he was living at home.

It is likely that this reflects some general bias of interest in the two key groups of professionals concerned, the health visitors and social workers, which may have unfortunate implications in many cases of non-accidental injury in which the father or step-father is, at least explicitly, the abusing parent, as in the Simon Peacock case, where the father was rarely if ever seen. And whether the father is or is not known to be the abuser, the marital inter-action may be crucial in assessing the balance of risk to the child.

One of our respondents expressed concern about many cases in which parents exposed their children to danger whilst not necessarily deliberately inflicting injuries upon them. This matter is considered by Oliver (1977) and it is not easy to disentangle the factors which may be associated with such behaviour in parents. There were at least three conferences which we attended to which this observation might be relevant. The hypothesis is a kind of bridge between the oft recurring 'Did he fall or was he pushed?' question. It may be that some parents are so immature and possibly mentally handicapped that the normal child protection mechanisms by which ordinary parents foresee and forestall harm to their children simply do not operate. Oliver's review of the research shows how difficult it is to disentangle intellectual limitation from experiences of deprivation in the parents' own childhood which may affect their parenting capacity. Another, more contentious explanation, concerns the dominance in some parents of unconscious motivation to harm the child which results in a failure to take appropriate avoiding action. Whatever explanation is advanced, it is the detail of parent and child inter-action which enables us to pinpoint such relationships and to assess the danger to the children.

Lastly, the most difficult to convey, is the way in which this information is integrated. There has been much research into the factors associated with child abuse in the last ten years. The findings do not enable us to 'predict' with confidence that given the presence of such and such factors a child will be abused. For example, many parents who have been ill-treated themselves as children do not later ill-treat their own children; many who have experienced difficult pregnancies or births do not 'fail to bond', and so on. But where a child is known to have been abused by his parents or where there is a strong probability that it has happened, there are now some clusters of factors associated with abusing parents which may be helpful in deciding the right course of action, for example, the extent of the risk which the conference is taking in leaving a child at home.

One of the conference purposes is to bring these together. Sometimes this was achieved. At other times there were gaps or mysteries. It is inevitable that with some families, and at some stages in the investigation, there will be such missing links. This is not necessarily a criticism of the workers, since it is well known that family situations in cases of child abuse are often ambiguous and sometimes accompanied by a lack of candour. It would be helpful, however, for the gaps and mysteries to be clearly defined *as such* towards the end of the conference. This did not always occur. To know which parts of the jigsaw puzzle are missing or do not fit may be reassuring and clarification to those present may give a focus for further investigations. It also avoids a kind of false synthesis, whereby the awkwardness of missing and ambiguous information are overlooked in an attempt by the group to achieve a satisfactory outcome.

From the above, it can be seen how complex a task confronts a case conference when one small group seeks to understand another (the family) by pooling information. Whilst there is no such thing as the complete picture, since family inter-action must necessarily be in part hidden from observers and can in any case be perceived and interpreted in many different ways and on many different levels, it is none the less salutory to remind ourselves how dependent the workers are on detailed, accurate observation if the treatment plan is to be appropriate. Sometimes a missing or distorted link can be seen to have affected the subsequent work. For example, in the Karen Spencer inquiry, the first case conference was given incorrect information about the circumstances surrounding Karen's birth. After an extremely difficult birth, in the course of which Karen was injured, she was separated from her mother for a month. The health visitor, it seems, volunteered the correct dates but 'the medical presentation of the case was to the effect that Karen's discharge was not delayed'. The chairman of the committee commented: 'The consultant paediatrician seems to have remained of the opinion that these were the facts throughout the case. This means that no attention was paid to a crucial period of separation and no inquiries were made of the hospital staff' (Karen Spencer, 1978, p. 8). Given the growing volume of research which suggests the relevance of pregnancy, birth and the post-natal period to subsequent bonding and the inter-action between mother and child, such a slip is clearly of major importance in failing to establish a complete picture on which to rest a plan of action.

DECISION MAKING

The second conference purpose which we proposed concerned decisions as to action. Our respondents' answers to, and questions about, this matter were somewhat confused, even ambivalent. Their comments raise the central issue of the function of the conference *per se*. Is it an advisory or executive body? Jones, McClean and Vobe (1978) draw attention to this. They comment that there is confusion; a government letter (DHSS, 1974) refers to 'the collective decisions' of the conference. Its advice, however, is blurred since it is suggested that 'the case conference should retain overall concern' (note, not responsibility) 'for the management of the case'. Jones *et al.* suggest that 'this confusion can be resolved if the conference is seen as advisory rather than executive'. It is clear that various agencies, especially those with specific statutory powers and duties, cannot in the last resort accept a conference recommendation as binding. Government advice (DHSS, 1976a, p. v) is specific on this point:

It is acknowledged that the decision of the case conference cannot be binding on the representatives of bodies with statutory powers and duties in relation to children and that, where a consensus view cannot be reached, any participant may, after consultation with senior officers, find himself constrained to take action contrary to that recommended by other members of the case conference. When this occurs, we urge that the other members be notified of the proposed action and reasons for disagreement, before such action is taken unless an emergency demands otherwise.

But to argue from that, that the conference is advisory does not, it seems to us, deal adequately with the complex interaction between the decision of the agencies and the conference. Government guidelines, followed by various inquiries, assume that the conference is a crucial part of case management. It is in no sense an 'optional extra' and, as we have discussed earlier, failure to call or to attend a conference may now be a cause for critical comment. Furthermore, it is interesting to note the emphasis in the above quotation on explaining, even justifying, to the conference the reasons for not following through conference plans. Thus a fieldworker is likely to feel some obligation to explain himself to the other participants if she/he goes against a conference decision.

In short, we are moving towards a situation in which a group of professionals coming together for a particular purpose constitute themselves as a decision-making body in some, but not all, the matters under debate. This interesting development has far-reaching implications for inter-organisational structures and relationships in the helping professions. It is not surprising, therefore, that our respondents' answers to our questions about these matters were generally uncertain. It was generally agreed that, formally, it was for the conference to decide upon the prime worker and whether a child should be placed on, remain on, or be removed from the at risk register. It was further generally agreed that it must usually be for social services to decide upon legal action to remove a child from home. (The NSPCC or police also have such powers.) The answers to the questions reflected two different strands of feeling, the first held quite strongly by those respondents who were not field social workers or their seniors. They were insistent that they were thankful for social services to have the main responsibility for decision making: 'I would dislike decision taking, so personally I am pleased.' This was strengthened by those who felt that they should not be asked to take such decisions, for example: 'My deputy felt it was an awful burden on her asking whether a child should stay on the register.' The uncertainty of those who are not familiar with the procedures, as one respondent who was not sure whether to place a child on the at risk register meant his removal from home and another similarly unsure about the consequences of a place of safety order, added to the anxiety and doubt about playing a part in conference decisions: 'I felt I was the only one there that really didn't want to see him moved (from home) and that it would be terrible if I was wrong.'

The other side of the coin, however, was resentment that social services had got everything 'tied up' beforehand. Some respondents felt that the conference was a bit of a charade so far as decisions were concerned. To be fair, this was confirmed, to an extent, by some social workers interviewed, who accepted that ultimate responsibility did rest with social services; two social workers, when pressed, said that if a conference did not wish to put a child on the register but the social workers did not agree with the decision, they would still have to reserve the right to visit as often as they thought appropriate.

Social services respondents were even clearer that the decision of a case conference about legal action would have to be 'reviewed' by social services. (A similar reservation was expressed by a police respondent and the NSPCC.) One doctor commented: 'Are case conferences being used as the conscience of social services? There must be a case conference so that social services, on whom blame is so frequently laid, can be seen to have discussed it with all concerned.' This respondent was *not*, however, implying that there was anything 'phoney' about the process. Rather, it was a question of some sharing of accountability.

What seems to emerge is that there is an urgent need to clarify the status of the conference in relation to different types of decision, to avoid implications of insincerity when the problem may really be that the distinction between advisory and executive responsibility is blurred. However, two other factors need to be taken into account. One is that, by sheer weight of numbers, social services may appear to hold greater power in the conference. (The different roles held by those present from social services were by no means clear to all respondents.) The second is that it might be helpful to make explicit to those who are only peripherally involved, or who are inexperienced, that they are not necessarily expected to give a decision on such matters as the at risk register if they are uneasy about doing so.

GATHERING EVIDENCE FOR USE IN
LEGAL PROCEEDINGS

Of the conferences we attended, in only three was the gathering of evidence with a view to court proceedings an explicit conference task, although the possibility lurked in some others. In one, at which a decision was made to take a place of safety order that day, the social services had been denied entry and therefore the evidence of others, above all the school teachers', was crucial. Because of the concern which had existed previously, the teachers had kept a careful note day by day of the condition of the children. The conference had been requested by the teachers following further episodes of physical injury. Thus the emphasis was on the need and justification for a place of safety order and subsequent care proceedings. This in one sense simplified the exchanges. The primary purpose was clear and the role of the senior officer from social services, who had attended, was to advise on the strength of the evidence in relation to possible care proceedings, as well as to raise questions concerning police involvement.

The position in the other two cases was much less clearcut. The family circumstances and the nature of the risk were complex so that discussion about evidence was much more difficult. In formulating the four 'conference purposes', we separated evidence from other forms of information to emphasise that this aspect of conference activity has certain special characteristics which may affect the attitudes and communications of those present. Although we have not many examples to draw upon from our study, it seems likely that difficulties do arise if the gathering of evidence is confused with more general sharing of information. Once the possibility of legal proceedings is on the agenda of the conference, a new kind of question is in the minds of the participants, especially those in social services who may have to take the case to court: 'Will the evidence stand up?' Inevitably, more attention is then paid to the hard facts, dates, 'incidents' and so on. Whilst this may be salutary, reminding those present of the dangers of over hasty conclusions and too much speculation, it is also important for participants to feel free to discuss subtler aspects of family inter-action for in so doing they may reach a different kind of truth which is just as important for long-term case management. For example, the quality of maternal affection, elusive as this may be, may be more significant for long term planning than the precise nature of injuries received. It is important, therefore, that those, be they lawyers or social services officers, whose task it is to draw attention to legal proceedings, do not allow these considerations to dominate the conference exchanges—they are present to advise and not to control the proceedings. Recently, in resolutions from an influential group which came together to formulate policies concerning child abuse (Franklin, 1977a, p. 197) we read: 'the local social services department should make available experienced legal advice at every case conference at which the legal position of any of the parties is to be considered.' We are doubtful about this suggestion, mainly because of the difficulties of drawing the line sensibly and defining situations *in advance* at which 'the legal position . . . is to be considered'. It sounds altogether too vague and may result in many more hours of professional time being spent unnecessarily in conferences. Furthermore, the effect of the legal presence should not be underestimated. We had a particularly vivid example of this at the only conference at which a legal representative from the County Secretary's Department was present. At that conference, the health visitor, in following the agreed policy of the professional association that evidence should be given only when subpoenas were issued, was in some considerable difficulty as to what to say. We do not know how often this leads to such difficulties. Some health visitors and nursing officers told us that social services departments understood the reluctance of health visitors to give evidence and would only call them when absolutely necessary. Yet other representatives of social services departments seemed unaware of the health visitor's position on this. It seems important to be clear whether a health visitor's silence in a conference represents a wish to avoid being subpoenaed, or that she agrees with what is being said, or that she simply does not have strong views on the point under discussion. However, perhaps the most important matter of all is the way in which the chairperson uses the legal representative; above all, participants should not feel that their observations are less valued if they are not perceived to be relevant to the legal process.

SHARING AND DIFFUSING ANXIETY

The fourth purpose of the conference, which has been little discussed in the literature, concerns the sharing of anxiety. This is a complicated matter and one which moves us into the area of process which is further discussed in the next chapter. So far as conference purpose is concerned, it should be said that the conference may, quite properly, increase or decrease anxiety as information is pooled. Obviously, it is no criticism of the conference if people leave it with an increased level of concern, suspicion and hence anxiety about the situation. Even when it is increased in one way, there may be relief that a problem has been faced, clarified and shared even if it proves to be as bad or worse than when the worker arrived. The conference is a forum in which anxiety may be appropriately or inappropriately raised. Thus, in one we attended, although the atmosphere was charged with anxiety, the consensus amongst members and the controlled quiet chairing left us in little doubt that as far as professional communication was concerned, the participants would leave it feeling 'OK' about each other. There were other similar examples, although, because the urgency of the situation was not so great, the issue was not so vividly highlighted. In contrast, there were some conferences at which the presenting problem was not such as to arouse intense realistic anxiety and yet the atmosphere was, to put it mildly, somewhat charged. The important question is: 'Why is this?' One must allow for past history concerning this or other cases and the professional inter-action which has resulted. People enter the room with views about the case and feelings about each other, sometimes strongly held. This was undoubtedly crucial to the dissatisfaction expressed by most of the participants whom we interviewed from two con-ferences. However, as we discuss later, the chairperson plays a crucial part in determining to what extent it is appropriate and helpful to bring out underlying conflicts of view and attitude, which in some instances created a tense atmosphere and inhibited genuine sharing of feelings. On the whole, the chairpersons did not do this; whether they should or not is an important matter to consider.

　　Whilst taking full account of this realistic anxiety which con-ferences about child abuse necessarily raise, it is important to acknowledge also the strands that raise or lower the temperature of such encounters. First, anxiety is to an extent contagious and the presence in a group of one member who is perhaps excessively anxious will affect other participants. The ways in which such anxiety is demonstrated and 'caught' by others are many and various and may alter the instrumental balance of the meeting. (For example, a defence against an over-anxious member may be to underestimate the significance of the observations, 'it's only Mrs X fussing again'.) Secondly, anxiety may be directly related to the circumstances of the case, even if it is excessive, or it may be a reflection of the burden of responsibility and accountability which a particular worker finds too heavy to bear. If the conference is to be more than a formality, the acknowledgement of such feelings explicitly or implicitly as, for example, when some plan involving support for such a worker is put forward, is very important. Group support may be mobilised. Sadly, the converse, when participants man their own barricades, is not uncommon. We would wish to argue that, however it is done, it is a conference task to face the anxiety engendered by such cases and to seek to find appropriate ways of managing it, although this does not relieve individual agencies of their responsibilities in this matter.

Consideration of the 'mood' of conferences, and the extent to which conference participants should recognise and seek to channel these feelings in order better to understand the needs and problems of the families they serve, leads us into a discussion of the *processes* of communication at conferences, the subject of the next chapter.

NOTES

1 Lambeth, Southwark and Lewisham Area Health Authority (Teaching) and London Boroughs of Lambeth, Southwark and Lewisham *Child Abuse: procedures in relation to non-accidental injury to children* (1975).

2 Our sample included more children of school age than might have been predicted, probably because it took place in July when school holidays were looming. It is likely that had it taken place at a different time there would have been more 'failures to thrive' and perhaps also more concern about general neglect of very young children.

Chapter 4

Case Conferences – the Processes

Some of the wider issues concerning the perceptions which professionals have of themselves and of each other are discussed in Chapter 2. These obviously affect the participants at case conferences, each of whom approaches the other with attitudes derived from varying mixtures of past experiences, favourable and unfavourable, and stereotypes (more often negative). The dynamics of the conference *per se*, therefore, have to be considered in this wider context. However, there are matters related to communication which the conference highlights with particular clarity.

The conference is a group in action. It may at first sight seem surprising that little attention has been paid to this obvious fact by the social workers who convene and participate in so many conferences, given that their training draws attention to group phenomena. However, this is part of a wider puzzle, for it seems that social workers do not generally relate this knowledge to their working groups. Our research concerning the task of the local authority social worker (DHSS, 1978) confirms this in relation to social service teams which are so crucial to effective service delivery. Questions are raised by Parsloe in this report concerning the extent to which the one-to-one model of social work practice is reinforced by failure to use the student group as such for learning (pp. 346-52). These team studies suggest that, whatever the reason, social workers are relatively unsophisticated in their thinking about, and use of, teams. The fact that the dynamics of the case conference have not received much scrutiny may, therefore, be better understood in this general context.

In this book we can do no more than suggest that this is a matter which would merit further investigation. The context in which this group inter-action takes place is unusual and will heighten some of the tensions inherent in group encounters. Some facts concerning the case conference make some of its special characteristics clear.

First, the conference members are drawn together by a common concern and anxiety about the welfare of a child, usually focused upon his physical safety. Thus, the subject is linked to one of our most powerful emotions concerning the protection of children.

Secondly, the safety of the child is endangered by the action or neglect of his parents or care-takers. This sharpens the intensity of the emotions and of the internal conflict of those present. However knowledgeable we may be, there are, at a deep level, feelings of anger and revulsion. These may be related to anxiety about our own potentiality for aggression towards those we love, especially those who are most dependent upon us. There are welcome signs that it is becoming more socially acceptable to admit to such negative feelings; for example, an ordinary mother's exasperation and anger with a fractious infant, accompanied by an urge to punish physically, is now acknowledged by many when they are in a climate conducive to such admissions. (We have further to go in admitting to such feelings about others, such as elderly dependent relatives.) But for many of us, to be faced with the harsh reality of ill-treatment of a child is a frightening reminder of aspects of ourselves that we would prefer not to acknowledge. In any case, such outraged feelings are a healthy basic response, a social mechanism for the protection of the dependent. The professional role, however, complicates our reactions still further. Some self-restraint and objectivity are expected in the performance of the professional task. Yet this has to spring from a degree of understanding and, perhaps, self-awareness. If it is simply a 'top dressing', negative feelings towards parents will persist and will, in various and subtle ways, affect the dynamics of the communications at the conference. A further complication is that not all the conference participants are likely to be professionally sophisticated in such matters. For those who may not have met child abuse before, participating in a conference may be emotionally painful to a greater degree than for others who are more experienced. If the conference is to achieve fruitful communication, the sensitivity of the group to such reactions from certain individuals and the way in which others, especially the chairperson, respond to them, may be crucial.

An illustration of the complex and intense feelings generated even in those who are experienced in the field is given in the description of the proceedings of the conference sponsored by the Royal Society of Medicine (Franklin, 1977a). A simulated case conference was held during the workshop and was said to have had 'a profound and disturbing effect on the audience'. The chairperson, in his report of the proceedings, added (p. 280):

The conclusions of the case conference are omitted from this account . . . They were severely criticised at each stage. Many critics heatedly proposed alternative solutions. When the temperature of the meeting fell to normal once more, many of these criticisms were seen to be without real foundation and the protagonists acting out of their own insecurity and the unease intimately connected with the making of decisions in these complex family situations.

One mechanism of defence merits special mention, that of denial. Early writers on the subject of child abuse drew attention to the fact that the medical profession generally had difficulty in accepting that certain types of injury could only have been caused by deliberate acts of parents or care-takers. Doctors are not alone in this and the refusal to draw the only possible conclusion in certain circumstances shows how deep rooted our resistances are. It is probably true to say that the professionals, whose work brings them in frequent contact with the problem and who have been exposed to so much discussion of it, are now less likely to deny the implications of certain injuries. But at a case conference, there will be others, for example, GPs and teachers, for whom contact with such cases is most infrequent. The possibility, therefore, of defensive denial is perhaps greater with such participants. However, the degree of emotional involvement of other workers with parents is another important factor in such denial, especially when there is a natural reluctance to admit that 'treatment' has failed. At one case conference we attended, the discussion was focused on the suggestion that a boy should be taken off the at risk register. There was no doubt that the father, a PT instructor, had seriously assaulted his step-son, some three years previously. Whilst there had been no further incidents and the relationship between father and step-son was thought to have improved, it was necessary for the chairperson of the case conference to remind the head teacher several times, gently but firmly, that there had been serious injuries to a boy who was not, like his father, physically robust. It seemed as if the head teacher wished to brush this aside altogether, having established a constructive relationship with the father in connection with school sport.

Thirdly, the participants do not usually start as a group confident in each other's roles and skills. More commonly, there is a fair degree of ignorance/mistrust of each other in relation to this highly charged issue. As has been pointed out earlier, they are not 'a team', even though a great deal of the discussion about interprofessional co-operation has centred upon this concept.

Fourthly, to a greater or lesser extent, participants are aware of their own responsibility and accountability. The group is not there simply to talk, to share information, but to formulate a management plan which will protect the child. Failure to do so may lead to tragedy for the family and criticism of some of the group members in a matter of the greatest professional and personal sensitivity.

Fifthly, in most instances, the case under discussion is only one part of the participants' busy working life. It demands priority, yet this has to be balanced against other priorities. It is likely that the participant will be acutely aware of this, the more so if his work requires him to spread himself thinly across a large number of people and problems. The position, for example, of a health visitor in this respect is very different from that of an NSPCC worker in a special unit.

Sixthly, the participants do not share a common background, in terms of general education, professional training, experience or agency structure. They have to find ways of talking to each other meaningfully in an hour or two, without the kind of shorthand that is used by those who share a knowledge base or frame of reference.

Lastly, as Dingwall (1978) has pointed out, the case conference involves a more formal and public interaction than many other situations in which professionals meet. It is likely, therefore, that occupational identity and authority is 'on-display', a point to which we shall return in considering some aspects of conference dynamics. The possibility that one might be involved in legal proceedings and the effect which this may have on participation reinforces the 'public' aspects of the occasion.

These are not the only important factors affecting the dynamics of the case conference. But even in listing seven of them, the complexities are highlighted. It is to be hoped that professionals, including social workers, whose business is to seek to understand such group processes in other contexts such as the family will extend their interest to the functioning of this work group, unusual as it is both in its purpose and its composition.

The literature on behaviour in small groups is prolific. Kane (1975) reviews it usefully in relation to interprofessional teamwork generally. She comments (p. 32):

> In assembling material the collator is faced with overlapping ideas which, nevertheless, are couched in rather distinctive language belonging to the originating group...The welter of terminology confuses the reader attempting to find common conclusions in the work of the social psychologist, social group worker, sociologist and management theorist.

Furthermore, much of the social psychological research has been undertaken in quasi-laboratory conditions, to control the intervening variables. Problem solving has been addressed to relatively straightforward issues, unlike those of child abuse and neglect, and ones which do not arouse such intense emotions. Therefore, caution must be exercised in applying such material to the case conference. None the less there is a value in paying attention to some of the findings. Kane notes that 'the larger the group ... the more acceptable unresolved differences become' (p. 36) and that 'the extent to which a team member will accept the norms is influenced by his status in the group, which in turn may be influenced by his professional affiliation ... the more eager an individual is to belong to a group, the more he will conform to its norms' (p. 37).

Such observations, derived from empirical research, warn us to beware of a simplistic assumption that the holding of the case conference is bound to be beneficial in terms of decisions taken, a view to which some of the recent literature on the subject comes perilously near.

Hoffman (1965, pp. 101-32), reviews the literature concerning factors inhibiting and promoting effective problem solving. He points out the strong pressures towards uniformity which exist in small groups. 'The experimental evidence', he claims, 'is quite clear on this point.' Groups tend to produce unanimous decisions, and discussions tend to increase the uniformity of their members' individual judgements.' Furthermore, 'even on objective problems there is no guarantee that unanimity produces truth; in fact, there is very often little relationship between the two' (p. 101). However, 'pressures towards uniformity may be merely the result of the typical experimental situation. The experimental conditions may have made the subjects think that the proper performance as subjects required them to arrive at a single solution to the problem. In real life, on the other hand, there is often very little motivation to arrive at a unanimous decision, but just how often is hard to tell and worthy of study ... pressures toward opinion uniformity may be detrimental to the group's effectiveness if it prevents search for and discussion of alternative possibilities' (p. 102).

One has only to reflect upon the matters upon which case conferences are called to agree, such as whether the child should remain at home, be removed or return home, to see the relevance of this research and the need for further examination of its validity in the naturalistic setting of the case conference.

Heslin and Dunphy (1964, pp. 99-112) discuss the significance of 'status consensus' in decision making in small groups. They report on thirteen studies whose findings 'support the notion that status consensus is an important dimension underlying variations in member satisfaction'. They point out that status consensus and hence member satisfaction 'will tend to be low where there is competition for leadership status, especially where competition leads to factionalism or clique-ishness', a suggestion that links with Dingwall's observation, mentioned earlier, that occupational identity is on public view at the case conference. The acceptability and competence of the chairperson at case conferences, especially in relation to the interaction between the medical and social welfare professionals, illustrates vividly the issue of status consensus.

Heslin and Dunphy (1964, pp. 99-112) consider other significant issues also relevant to our theme. They discuss the apparent discrepancy of research findings concerning member satisfaction as between the 'wheel and circle' modes of participation. The results of different studies appear contradictory, suggesting that some groups are more satisfied with the wheel and spoke model, in which interaction moves to and from the centre, others with maximum inter-action between members, as in a circle. Drawing attention to the varied groups studied by the different researchers, they point out:

> The clue to their divergent results . . . appears to lie in the differing expectation of members about the extent to which they can and should legitimately participate. If they feel free to fulfill their expectations about participation, satisfaction will be high.

The authors suggest that in studies of conferences of executives in business and government 'junior or less knowledgeable members would expect to participate to a lesser degree.' This was apparent in our own study of conferences, in which some who were either inexperienced or may have perceived themselves as of lower status, told us that they only spoke when spoken to. Our case conference research shows a wide variety of professional experience both in general and in relation to child abuse specifically. This complicates the inter-action of members; the typical case conference will be a mixture of 'wheels and circles' and individual member satisfactions will depend on their differing expectations.

Hoffman (1965, p. 108) discusses the related issue of power structure in groups; studies demonstrate that although these structures may mitigate 'the negative effects of personality factors', they 'may also create new barriers to effective problem solving'. He writes:

> The presence of authority relations in a group seems to change

the character of the discussion. There is a greater concentration on the ideas of the high status person and the group has to spend considerable time either supporting or rejecting his views rather than searching for alternatives.

Such observations have considerable implications for the process of the case conference, both for the way in which chairpersons play their parts and also for those whose professional authority is brought into the group; for example, the paediatrician, in communication with nurses, health visitors and so on, forms a subgroup, with its own internal power relations not necessarily shared by others present.

Matters concerned with leadership and authority are further considered by Berkowitz (1953, pp. 231-8). He examines group cohesiveness, satisfaction and productivity in relation to the performance of the leadership role. The general finding, that group cohesiveness may be lessened by leadership sharing, interestingly does not apply when problems are relatively urgent. Then 'not only does leadership sharing fail to lessen cohesiveness and member satisfaction . . . but the leader's permissiveness and the proposing of solutions by the members tend to make for more attractive group situations.' Case conferences vary greatly in their urgency; they are on a continuum from those in which a life and death situation exists and a decision must be taken at once, to those which form part of an on-going case management and are, in fact, a review of progress. It would seem from what Berkowitz says, therefore, that a group of people, similar or identical in composition, meeting at various times for different purposes but in relation to the same case may respond differently at different times to the same style of leadership.

We must add that the relationship between member satisfaction and the quality of the decision making is complex. Pressure to conformity on the one hand, status conflict within the group on the other, are two examples of the group dynamics which could adversely affect the quality of decisions, which are, in any case, difficult to evaluate objectively on such complex issues. Clearly, the satisfaction of those members who are required to implement the conference decisions is important, since their commitment will affect their attitudes to the management plan. The risks of unconvinced action are ones to which conference participants, especially the chairperson, need to be alert.

The foregoing comments are intended simply to illustrate the potentiality of the study of groups, for our understanding of the case conference process. They raise as many as or more questions than they answer but the central place occupied by the case conference in British child abuse and neglect procedures justifies its examination from various theoretical perspectives, of which this aspect of psychology is one.

Another aspect of communication in which we became particularly interested following our observation of the conferences, concerns the use of specialised knowledge/jargon. Although the word 'jargon' is often used pejoratively, to describe obscure, even mystifying language, it need not carry such implications. Every occupational group has its own shorthand, words (or frequently nowadays initials of which NAI, Non Accidental Injury, is a topical example) which make sense if one is part of that group. Jargon, therefore, can be economical and an effective means of communication. The problem for the case conference participants is that they do not all share this common language. Several occupational groups were present; with and between them were differing amounts of experience and familiarity with child abuse. It was, therefore, not easy to assess in the conferences we observed how much was generally understood of technical contributions. On no occasion did members during the conference seek clarification of technical points about which they might have been unclear. The interviews with participants explored the extent to which technical or specialised exchanges had been understood and whether or not people had felt able to ask when unsure.

The information gained from the interviews about this is difficult to analyse since we gained an impression of vague and slightly evasive answers to the questions. This could suggest that respondents found as much difficulty in admitting uncertainty to us as they seemed to have done in the conference. A number commented that while they thought *they* had *broadly* understood, they imagined that many others present would not have done. We had some difficulty in pursuing these questions as we did not wish to give the impression of testing respondents. When pressed, however, some acknowledged that they did not find it easy to ask for clarification of things they had not understood in conferences: 'No, I don't find it easy to say "Would you like to explain in simple language what that means?".'

The three main types of technical contribution in the conferences were medical reports, the law relating to children and the predictors and signs of child abuse. On several occasions in the conference medical information was presented in technical language apparently not understood by all those present. For example, one account of the findings on clinical examination of a child admitted to hospital with suspected non-accidental injury used medical shorthand concerning bruises etc. Although at the end of the presentation 'the message' was generally clear, we believe that the impression made on the non-medical members was of being baffled by science.

One topic, not perhaps of paramount importance to the conference, none the less illustrates well a number of problems arising from technical contributions. It concerns a doctor's account of a child's hearing problem and involved the unusual phrase 'glue and grommets'. The pertinent issue for those present was not to understand the finer details of how the 'glue', accumulating in the child's ears causing hearing loss, had been treated by the insertion of 'grommets', but rather whether this problem would have been picked up earlier by a more caring and concerned mother and whether there was any residual hearing loss after treatment likely to affect the child's future schooling or behaviour in the home. Interviews with those who had heard and at times misunderstood this contribution were interesting. The doctor concerned held the view that:

> any professional can communicate what he's talking about to non-professionals, if he wants to, presuming he's intelligent and an adequate professional and doesn't feel threatened, or feel 'if I let people into the simplicity of my secrets then I'll have no status'. Most professional things are very simple.

And simple enough they were when an explanation was given in the follow-up interview. He argued that it was a function of the chairperson to seek clarification for the group as a whole if this seemed necessary. Some of those present said they had understood this information and confirmed that they would have asked if they had not; others admitted to some confusion. One said that she had discussed the problem beforehand with the health visitor and had she not done so 'I would have been very lost because I didn't understand the technical terms'. The quotation below illustrates that one of the difficulties is recognising a need to ask! 'Glue? These were things the kid had put in his own ears. Yes, I understood. I'd have queried it if I didn't—or somebody would.'

More serious than this somewhat frivolous example was uncertainty or confusion about the technicalities of the law relating to children and of the broader legal framework within which social services departments have to operate in respect of children at risk. It was clear that the precise implications of phrases such as 'place of safety order', 'reception into care', 'Section 2 rights' etc. were not always understood by all of those present. Yet these terms were often central to the debate at the conferences and it was important for them to be clearly understood if all present were to share fully in making recommendations or taking decisions. To take just one example from many: at a conference called to discuss proceedings following a place of safety order one of the participants, who disclosed in a subsequent interview that she was opposed to the removal of the child from the home, believed that care proceedings would automatically follow a place of safety order and was unaware that the child could, in fact, have been returned home.

Some of those interviewed spoke openly about their uncertainty regarding the law saying that they left it to 'the professionals'—the social workers. Others were less sure, and implied that they felt they should know more of this than they did, for example: 'I feel guilty about that. One sometimes says something ought to be done but one doesn't really know what the legal rights are.' Some of the social services representatives seemed to think that the legal terms were more 'self-explanatory' than in fact proved to be the case, but others recognised the difficulties and were uncertain as to how best to explain the legal position in the case conferences. They were worried about appearing too didactic from the chair or taking up valuable time. Yet several people spoke of the greater attention given recently to the teaching of law, in basic and in-service training courses for health visitors, for example, but acknowledged that it was easier to learn when it was applied to particular cases than 'in theory'. One said:

> 'Well, we had a course and I've probably got a booklet somewhere that I should be reading which would explain it all no doubt—but I find it easier, quite honestly, to pick up these meanings as you're working and involved than it is to sit down and read a book and think what is that all about?'.

It was clear that several people (some doctors, nursery school supervisors, nursing officers) had indeed acquired a thorough working knowledge of the relevant law precisely in this way through applying it to particular cases.

Possibly the most important and complex area of communication concerns predictors and signs of child abuse. There are two particular difficulties at conferences. First, the technical knowledge of the participants varies greatly; many conferences include a teacher or playgroup leader who have not met the problem before and to whom the discussion of signs and their significance is entirely foreign. Others present, such as perhaps the health visitor or probation officer, will have encountered the problem before but infrequently. Yet others, such as a specialist social worker in social services or from NSPCC special units, may be extremely knowledgeable and experienced, as are certain paediatricians and hospital based social workers with a particular interest in the subject. This places a heavy burden on the conference chairperson (although the other participants are not exempt from responsibility for asking or explaining) to ensure that participants are 'hearing' the information presented in the same way.

At the conferences we attended, it was our impression that there was greater clarity about physical signs of abuse than about the more intangible aspects related to the 'feel' of the parent/child inter-action, even when these might be relevant to the possibility of physical abuse. When information about the family dynamics was shared at conferences it was unclear whether all those present perceived the clues in the same way. In one conference, to take a simple example, a mother suspected of having injured her child was referred to several times by the social worker as 'young'. It was not clear whether this was repeated often in the expectation that those present would draw a particular inference from the fact or simply as a description akin to 'the mother is short or dark' or whatever. Another example was when a social worker voiced her anxieties about the way in which a mother was holding her baby and a health visitor suggested that the mother would be unlikely to hold the baby close to her after a caesarian section. Again, the inference to be drawn from this was not spelled out and one nursing officer suggested that health visitors may in the past have been too modest about the inferences they are particularly qualified to draw from their observation. Certainly there was an impression at some conferences of significant pieces of information 'left hanging in the air'.

A second, and in some ways more important aspect, concerns the difficulty, not simply of explaining the significance of certain information to less knowledgeable members but of an appraisal of the status of the research evidence, so that the weight to be given to information about a specific family is considered at the conference. Much effort has recently been made to acquaint those likely to deal with cases of child abuse with the relevant signs and predictors. Several of those interviewed mentioned study days and written information designed to plug the gaps left for many in their basic training. One respondent pin-pointed a danger, however, when he said: 'We are all under the illusion that everybody knows everything at the moment because there's been so much.' But the fact is that the research into this problem has proliferated in the last decade, not only in the UK but internationally, especially in the

USA. Most of it is concerned with the aetiology and diagnostic aspects. We have reached a point when very few professionals, even those who specialise in this area of work, can claim with confidence that they are up to date with, and able to interpret, the significance of the research findings. A particular danger, as has been mentioned earlier, lies in the use of information concerning the situation of the parents which does not necessarily single them out from thousands or millions of their contemporaries, until it is placed alongside more unusual happenings. Thus, talk of housing problems, unemployment, single parents, step-parents amongst abusing parents has to be put in the context of all the other parents similarly situated who do not injure their children.

We have suggested earlier that it may be helpful to think in terms of clusters of factors, in which a combination of environmental stress, childhood experiences of the parents and the present interactions conspire to increase the risk to certain children, and that integrating this information is a primary task for the conference. Knowledge of research findings should affect the way that this is done, but they can only be used to inform the exercise of professional judgement. In any case, in a field of study so recent and so prolific, today's accepted wisdom is likely to be rejected tomorrow. A timelag between researchers and practitioners, especially those who are not specialists, is inevitable. Perhaps of more concern is the probability of distortion of what evidence is currently available when knowledge is 'picked up' from occasional attendance at conferences. It could, therefore, be argued that great effort should be made to ensure that at least the chairperson is given the time and opportunity to keep up to date with the research which should inform professional judgements. How they should do so is again problematical, given the quantity and variable quality of the research. This is surely a matter in which central government, in particular the DHSS, or professional associations should act as 'filters' for practitioners.

From the foregoing it will be seen that the role of the chairperson is of great importance in ensuring that conference purposes are carried out by effective control of its processes. From our observations, we came to the conclusion that it was the single most important factor in the success or failure of the conference, a view which is supported in a recent paper by Jones, McClean and Vobe (1978, p. 5) who write in describing conferences in Nottinghamshire: 'Chairmen were identified as crucial to the system and a working party was established to devise guidance and training. Management consultants have long recognised the importance of chairmanship training but this is still comparatively new to social work agencies.'

At the time of our research little had been written about the role
and those whom we interviewed had not thought much about it,
although, when questioned, there was a considerable consensus as
to the qualities required for good 'chairing'. The chairpersons
whom we interviewed varied considerably in their confidence about
the task, some expressing anxiety about the role and about the
balance needed between control and permissiveness. Our own
observations suggested that the styles and skills of the thirteen
varied considerably.

Of the thirteen conferences, ten were clearly and unequivocally
chaired by representatives of social services, who were either area
officers, divisional co-ordinators, or their representatives; in the
two conferences held in hospitals there appeared to be some confusion, confirmed by the participants at one who gave us different
answers as to who had been the chairperson. Castle (1976) shows
that 72 per cent of the conferences surveyed by the NSPCC were
chaired by senior staff of social services departments and 12 per
cent by hospital consultants. It would seem, therefore, that our
study had roughly the same percentage of social services officers in
the chair as might have been expected from the national figures.
But although social services carry major responsibility for this,
others, especially doctors, carry a share, particularly when conferences are held in hospital. It would be interesting to know how
often the hospital conferences give rise to the confusion which we
observed.

It highlights the long-standing and as yet unresolved problem
which has two facets; the actual and the perceived authority of the
medical profession in relation to other groups. This is not to
suggest that it would not be appropriate for a doctor to chair such a
conference. In certain circumstances, it may be the obvious course
and it could, in any case, be argued that it is the personal qualities
rather than the role which should determine the choice. (In
practice, this is very difficult to follow because of the invidious
distinctions between personalities which would then arise.) What
seems clear, however, is that whoever takes the chair should give
some consideration to the skills involved in performing the task. A
member of any profession will not, by virtue of *that* competence,
have the requisite abilities to chair a conference successfully.

Most of our respondents thought that it was appropriate for
social workers to take the chair because they had major responsibility: 'It's in their court . . . ', 'they are holding the baby', and so
on. Furthermore, there was quite a good level of satisfaction with
the chairperson's performance and high praise for one or two.
About half a dozen respondents, including those in social services,

commented on the possible disadvantage of a social services chair-person being *'parti pris'* and less independent than was desirable:

> It's usually social services that run the conference and it's usually the social services senior social worker who chairs it. I have found this rather unbalanced. I feel it needs someone totally impartial . . . I have found, though not at this conference, that very often everything is lined up before we get there and the chairman knows exactly what to ask because he knows all about the case *but he only knows about it from the social services point of view* (authors' italics).

All had difficulty in suggesting an alternative, though a DHSS social work service officer was proposed.

At one of the feedback discussions with the area review com-mittee, following our study, a social services representative argued strongly that 'independence' was not a desired attribute of those chairing case conferences and she expanded her views in a letter. An extract is quoted below:

> Whatever powers to remove a child some other agencies might have and exercise at a particular moment, *only* Social Services have the liability for on-going, adequate support and safeguard-ing of the child—at home or away, before and after the confer-ence and thus for constant reappraisal of a dynamic stage.
>
> Therefore, we have the profoundest motivation for ascertain-ing that all participants in the conference have explored and dis-played their observations clearly; have understood and modified each other's perceptions appropriately; have dealt with their feelings adequately enough to make realistic, individual contri-butions to the treatment plans; have committed themselves clearly to a particular undertaking. Those pieces of the jigsaw must add up to a conviction by the Social Services Department that removal of a child is or is not necessary, both today and as far henceforward as events and commitments remain con-stant.
>
> Whatever the theoretical possibility that GPs or Health Visitors might be legally and professionally competent to main-tain the case in the community on their own responsibility, my experience is that they want us to 'take charge' of the on-going surveillance and family support in any cases of substance. From time to time, when the child is in hospital, there is conflict about intentions to restore to or remove from home. In such cases, I consider it vital that the consultant should recognise our unique

responsibility about a child's safety and his welfare—through time; throughout his childhood.

In practice, when the chairmanship is not in the Social Services line manager's hands, conferences may stop short of explicating a diagnosis or treatment commitment—to our satisfaction.

In consequence, to avoid distortion of the content of any particular conference by unclarity of chairmanship or power struggles, I would heartily welcome an inter-agency policy recognising our role as chairman.

This raises a fundamental issue concerning the role of the chairperson; impartiality as between agencies would no longer be seen as so significant. Such a view supports the idea of 'an advisory conference' discussed earlier. If one does not accept that (and we do not) then the role of the chairperson is inevitably widened to include the mediating activities necessary to reach consensus. Some of our respondents tacitly accepted this. 'It's rather like being a member of the United Nations. You get beyond your own empire' indicates that some chairpersons accept a definition of role which takes them temporarily, as it were out of their agency.

We asked those of our respondents who chaired what tasks they thought were involved in the role. Not all mentioned the following points but the list compiled between them was fairly comprehensive. It included the following: to perform introductions; to give everybody present the opportunity of contributing information and of saying what they or their agency could offer; to control—to keep discussions relevant; to pull theories together, towards making a decision and a treatment plan; to help 'clear anxiety and to get it into the open, to put it on record and share responsibility'; to explain the law where necessary and to elucidate jargon.

Many of the qualities mentioned would of course be widely recognised as crucial to committee chairing generally. However, the case conference about child abuse highlights and exaggerates common tensions and problems. It is easy enough to list the tasks but hard to ensure that they are performed. It may be that in-service training for chairpersons might be developed and there are signs that this is taking place in some areas. There would seem to be five matters upon which such training might profitably be focused.

The first concerns the explanatory and educative functions of the chairperson. This ranges from simple matters such as introductions, to the elucidation of jargon and of the legal position.

Secondly, the chairperson has the ultimate responsibility for putting the pieces of the family jigsaw together and for ensuring that the participants have also, as it were, seen the complete jigsaw (and have seen which pieces are missing). One aspect of this skill is well illustrated in the following quotation:

> Very often people can have been working with the families for a very long time. When asked to give a picture of a husband or wife, they find it extremely difficult. I find myself asking specific questions like, 'How tall is he?' 'How big is he?' 'How does he receive you?' 'Does he ever nurse the children?' 'Does he cook?' 'Do you ever see him do the housework or is he never there?' 'Does he have a pint of beer?' and so on.

A third and exceedingly difficult task concerns the balance held between the control of irrelevance and the facilitating of communication. This has a bearing on the length of conferences. Castle (1976) found that 52 per cent of the conferences were between one and two hours in length and 5 per cent over two hours. A number of our respondents complained that the conferences went on too long. However, bearing in mind that the general educational levels and specific knowledge amongst the participants varied so greatly, it is not to be expected that all those present will be able to pinpoint quickly the salient factors of the case from their point of view. A certain amount of discursive, even anecdotal, material is, therefore, necessary in the early stages of the conference. The skill of the chairperson lies in utilising such contributions and drawing out from them the relevant points.

We have discussed earlier the conference as a medium for sharing, and at times, reducing anxiety. A wider aspect of this which the chairperson has to take into account concerns the airing of feelings at the conference. This is a controversial and yet important issue. When are feelings, either about the family or other professionals 'getting in the way' of rational discussion and decision making? How far is it the task of the chairperson to bring these out and in what manner? Are discussions sometimes initiated privately after conferences by chairpersons when tensions have run high between some participants? Should they be?

The final area for which the chairperson carries a heavy burden of responsibility concerns decision making. This involves taking the sense of the meeting (including an acknowledgement of dissent) and clarifying the issues that fall to be decided, or not to be decided, by the conference. In view of our earlier discussion concerning the somewhat blurred position of the conference poised somewhere between an executive and an advisory function, this is arguably the most important of the tasks of the chair if interprofessional confidence is to be generated and ill will avoided.

Our comments on chairing should not be taken to assume that in those conferences which we observed these skills were necessarily lacking. Indeed, we derived some of the suggestions from watching the task skilfully performed. However, it is fair to say that out of the thirteen, there was, in our view, considerable variation in the skills of management from the chair. It seemed that more help could and should be offered to those who take on this difficult and demanding role. It is no exaggeration to say that a child's life may depend in no small measure on the skills of the chairperson.

The conference is only one event in a sequence of activities concerned with communication between professionals. Some of our respondents stressed the importance of preliminary work which could make the conference more meaningful and efficient. One aspect of this is relevant to our earlier discussion of the missing pieces in the conference jigsaw—that is the possibility of consultation by the chairperson or prime worker with those who cannot be present but whose knowledge may be a vital link in the chain. We do not know how commonly this is done but at some of the conferences which we observed such information was not available. Our respondents confirmed the views expressed by Jones *et al.* (1978, p. 3): 'It would appear that those attending conferences rarely give much prior detailed thought to their contribution.' To us it was suggested that *within* professions, prior discussion between, say, senior and junior staff, might help the field staff concerned to clarify their views and then to present their points more clearly. This was emphasised by two nursing officers, who both said that, despite pressures on time, they tried to do this. Doctors also stressed that better prior preparations might lead to greater efficiency: 'A small number of people would achieve the same result—(professional) groups could get together beforehand.' (Certainly at the two hospital conferences we attended, there were rather a lot of doctors present. But it may be argued that their presence was an educational function.)

Another doctor put points about preparation very cogently:

> there is a horrible feeling that some people see the case conference as being what they are working towards and . . . sigh with relief—'Well, there'll be a case conference on Thursday' and don't spend Wednesday looking to see what hospital records they've got on the child, the siblings or . . . the parents. I feel it helps a lot if people go with their information coordinated. Even the people who are most concerned could go with an idea between them of what they want the management to be, rather than everybody . . . throwing in ideas and anxieties . . .

Jones, McClean and Vobe (1978, p. 3), whilst arguing against 'the presentation of voluminous written material', suggest that 'a page of relevant factual detail... can be valuable' and that 'each person should be able to present a summary of their involvement without constant reference to bulky files of ill-ordered notes' (a cry from the heart, this). Very few of the conferences we attended had written material of this kind although, as researchers, we were grateful for some background material made available to us to 'fill us in'. One participant thought the background was helpful as 'an *aide-memoire*' at each conference 'even if it were only the names and ages of family members and the dates of relevant events'. The work involved for the fieldworker and secretary is considerable but there remains a question—in some conferences, would the time of a group of busy people be more usefully employed if background updating information were presented in writing? This would seem a possibility where regular reviews were planned well in advance. An added advantage is that the very act of writing clarifies impressions. However, anxiety was expressed at the problems of confidentiality arising when written reports often containing sensitive information were circulated to conference members.

Preparation beforehand might tighten and focus the actual conference. Another crucial point was made by one respondent: 'There are so many things that come up in case conferences about which we should have a clear answer before we go. *You finish with a quarter of the people there and then have to send letters about the decision*' (authors' italics). It is hardly necessary to emphasise the dangers inherent in child abuse cases in this all too common committee phenomenon. Obviously, however, preparation of this kind may not be possible on a crisis conference. And it can be argued that such preliminary processes strengthen the feelings of pre-arranged plots, although the same doctors pointed out that this can be allayed if all those very closely involved can be consulted first. In any case, this cannot in our view over-ride the importance of such preparation if professional time is not to be wasted and the credibility of the conference as part of case management is to be maintained.

Recording of conference discussion is extremely important in the continuing communications between the professionals present, for those unable to attend or those whose presence may not be essential but who need by virtue of their accountability within their own agency to be kept informed. Jones, McClean and Vobe (1978, p. 3) put the case strongly:

A detailed, accurate account of decisions and discussion is

essential. The record is necessary as one factor in the assessment
of subsequent actions. Should things go wrong a record will be
required by an inquiry. Recording is a skilled task. Conferences
are . . . discursive and conjectural.

The authors argue for such recording to be done by social workers
'with special training and competence'. In our study, the practice
of minute taking varied greatly. Of our thirteen conferences,
minutes were taken by a secretary at four. We presume that the
social worker concerned was responsible for the rest, although, in
at least three, no one was taking notes 'publicly'. (We did not
receive minutes of all the conferences we attended but it would be
quite understandable if we were left off the circulation list, and we
do not infer from this that participants did not receive them.)

The minutes of the conferences taken by the secretary in one area
team were very full, a near verbatim note being taken of what
participants said. These were by far the most detailed and we were
interested in the reactions of the participants, which we gained
from our own interviews and that with the secretary. It seemed that
it had the effect of making the participants check their contribution
very carefully and, not infrequently, query statements they were
said to have made. The secretary commented on the difficulty of
minuting tones of voice.

One divisional co-ordinator only recorded in detail where there
was dissent. Two nursing officers told us that they kept their own
notes and checked these against minutes. Another participant was
worried about the possibility of slight distortions which could be
important. For example, she had said that a child had told her she
had been baby sitting *once* and this had turned up in the record as
'went baby sitting' as if it might be a frequent occurrence.

We would not wish to argue that it is in general more appropriate
for a secretary than a social worker to take the minutes, although
perhaps a compromise is for a social worker to construct them
from a shorthand taken by a secretary. Much will depend on the
talents of those who are available, whether administrative staff or
social workers. What *must* be emphasised, however, is that the
taking of minutes is a technique requiring skill and experience. It
does not follow that a social worker will do it well by virtue of
being a social worker. Above all, it is not in our view desirable that
the note be taken by the worker involved with the case. It is likely to
be done better by someone detached with regular and frequent
responsibilities for so doing.

There are some important issues behind this matter of minute
taking. One can be sure that the fuller the minute, the more queries

there will be as to shades of meaning and emphasis and we had evidence that there had been some ill feeling generated by minutes (though not of the conferences we attended). One nursing officer commented: 'The minute-taking is influenced by the attitude that is going on, the way it is said ... Their attitude comes over, rightly or wrongly, it comes out on paper.' This rightly emphasises the difficulty in objective recording, especially in situations where feelings are running high. If, as is sensible, the chairman and the minute taker are both from the same agency, usually social services, there is a responsibility on the chairman and minute taker to ensure that the balance of the record is fair. One way of doing this is to keep the record strictly factual, with perhaps only decisions recorded. But, if the conference is in part an exercise in shared accountability, then it can be argued that to record the observations and anxieties, and where these differ between the various workers is only fair.

Another aspect concerns confidentiality. Broadly speaking, the more paper there is, the harder it is to preserve confidentiality. One of our respondents, a head teacher, was very worried indeed about 'holding' detailed case material in school, which, she pointed out, was of quite a different nature from ordinary school records. All the major agencies will, no doubt, have policies regarding 'storage' of such material, but some discussion with those more peripherally involved might be helpful.

In our view, this matter of records and minutes merits further consideration. It seems clear that, if minutes are to be more than 'bare bones', then there is a need for some help and training for those taking them and for resources to be allocated to enable the job to be done well. Furthermore, some monitored experiments would be helpful. Some of the special units of the NSPCC have made a useful start in standardising recording in certain areas. But the practice over the country varies greatly and there are several unresolved questions as to what is the most appropriate way to record conference proceedings.

Since one of the prime purposes of conferences is to share information, one would expect that the issue of confidentiality would present significant difficulties. It is frequently referred to as a barrier to interprofessional communication. For example, the East Sussex County Council (1975, p. 19) response to the Colwell inquiry states:

> Every agency that was interviewed raised the question of confidentiality in one form or another. It was obvious that they all regarded this as a fundamental issue. There were said to be

special reasons for not passing on intensely personal information about children or parents . . . There is anxiety on the part of every profession that the information they disclose to others will be abused, either by being passed direct to the client and even to outsiders with unfortunate results, perhaps that it may be used insensitively as when a teacher makes a point of the fact that a child is adopted. It was apparent, however, that all the professions felt that when there was trust between them, particularly when individuals know and respect each other, less difficulties would arise from confidentiality. Face to face contact on a continuing basis produces an entirely different situation because it engenders trust and where there is trust there is a ready exchange of information.

Our study did not reveal such widespread concern as might have been predicted from these and many other statements to be found in the pages of professional journals. We are left wondering if our findings are atypical or whether this is an issue which, when probed, is found to be at once less substantial, less clear cut, and more complex than at first appears. Most of those interviewed thought that considerations of confidentiality did not, in practice, inhibit the sharing of information at conferences. Thus, if information was not freely shared, as at times it was not, it was usually for reasons other than confidentiality. These include the inhibiting effect of the size of the conference, uncertainty about the purpose of the conference, anxiety and tension between the participants. Early in the research one of those interviewed suggested that information was unlikely to be freely shared in multi-disciplinary gatherings and said: 'I'm pretty sure that at each case conference somebody is withholding something.' However, when those interviewed were asked about this proposition most said that they had not acted in this way nor did they usually think that others present had done so.

Some of those interviewed were impatient with the idea that any factors were preventing open communication between professionals in the conference they had attended, with comments such as: 'It's not in my nature to be inhibited'; 'I was happy with the sharing at the conference. I would speak up anyway', and 'I think all these people are professional and if they want to say something I think they ought to.' Some of the participants made a clear statement of their position on sharing information about their clients or patients in case conferences. A number stressed the difference between sharing responsibly in the conference and 'mere gossip'. One said of this:

I think that whatever I say in a conference is for the information of the people there to assist them in coming to a conclusion. They may bring out an aspect of something of which I am only on the periphery and I am able to bring to the conference another point of view and they can gain by it. But when you come away from the meeting the confidentiality must be kept within that small group of people who deal with it.

Several of those interviewed spoke of having sought permission from clients to share information in the interests of trying to help the family. For example:

I feel that anything that helps the child or the family (should be shared) and I always say to the parents, 'Now listen, you know that if I feel that this has to be taken to the right agency I would tell them.' I always tell them this before they start pouring it out.

Another equally explicitly said:

Confidentiality is very little of a problem. The families know and are told that they are being seen by a team of people and therefore they know and expect the information to be shared. Occasionally there will be things which they don't want to be generally known. It's very rare, but occasionally there are, and if it isn't of direct relevance for the safety of the child, then, of course, confidentiality is respected. I'm thinking particularly about marital problems and that kind of thing. However, if it has direct bearing on the safety of the child, then they will be told that this will have to be shared.

Marital problems, given as an example in the quotation above, were most frequently cited as the subject which would be mentioned but not normally discussed in intimate detail at a full conference.

A few teachers distinguished carefully between hard, observable facts about schooling and the child's behaviour in the school (which they would share) and other kinds of information (which they would not share) picked up through 'the local grapevine and because of the nature of things and, because grapevines do operate, a great deal of the family background is known in school.' The difficulty is that while the teachers showed a proper caution about spreading gossip, some knowledge about the family background, picked up on the 'grapevine', can, if properly understood and used, be very important in assessing the family situation—particularly as teachers may be the nearest to the 'community ear'.

The sensitivity and caution in this matter shown by these teachers is interesting since those interviewed had more reservations about sharing information with teachers than with any other group. This worry went beyond individual difficulties experienced by some in the past and was more deep seated. The concern seemed to be two-fold: first, that teachers might use the information inappropriately in their dealings with the children involved and, secondly, that written information might be stored without appropriate safeguards in schools.

This anxiety about teachers apart, most people argued, as did those interviewed in East Sussex, that sharing information was dependent upon trust in the particular personalities involved, often affected by previous dealings over the case under discussion or others, rather than considerations of role or agency. This was a difficult area for us to disentangle since, particularly at second or subsequent conferences, many of those involved had been working and meeting together more or less happily over months or years. The previous inter-action clearly affected the particular pieces of communication observed by us and in some cases it was plain that troubles in the past severely hampered a free exchange of information.

It is important to disentangle some of the threads running through these observations and some of the concerns commonly voiced by members of the professions. The medical profession features prominently in any discussion of confidentiality. For doctors, as for others, however, there is no absolute principle at stake. There may at times be conflicts of interests, especially if one member of the family, a parent, is a client. In such cases the child will often be the client of the same doctor but, even when this is not so, the doctor's ethical responsibility is clear. Dom Benedict Webb (1977, p. 238), cites Marshall as stating that there is an obligation on the part of the doctor to divulge some of the information obtained from his client 'when there is a possibility of serious harm to an innocent third party'. Furthermore, from a legal standpoint, the doctor, it would seem is also supported in disclosure of certain confidential information. Bevan reports (1975, p. 135), a legal opinion as follows:

On the narrow legal issue about confidentiality, you can take it that in practical terms there is really no possibility of the parent of any injured child obtaining any remedy against the doctor who participated in consultations of this kind. The confidential relationship . . . is . . . not an absolute one and a doctor is entitled to break the confidence in certain circumstances; one of these is where he feels under a social obligation to do so. There is the additional point that in these cases the practitioner also owes a duty of care to his patient (i.e. the child) and, by failing to participate in the consultation, he may be in breach of that duty of care.

In practice, therefore, the doctor is under no greater restraint than others, especially social workers. Ethical dilemmas will arise for both. Both may on occasion have to divulge information without the consent of the patient or client, which should obviously be obtained wherever possible. This may arise if the patient or client refuses permission, or if the circumstances are of such urgency that there is no time either to see the parents at all or (more likely) to work with them towards an understanding that it is necessary for the protection of their child to share the information.

The comments of our teacher respondents about 'gossip' remind us that how information is received depends on whether it is seen to be relevant to the understanding of the family's problems. In this, the doctor may be, on occasions, in a slightly easier position than social workers. He may be in possession of 'hard facts' concerning mental or physical health the relevance of some of which are readily accepted by conference participants. Others such as social workers will also have some such information which is of importance to the conference. But they may also have less tangible information and views about family circumstances, which are equally important but more open to misinterpretation and misunderstanding by participants who do not share the same frame of reference for understanding the problems. A further complication is the way in which words or phrases which should be morally neutral may be taken pejoratively. Phrases such as 'an immature mother' are particularly prone to this slide into moralising. (The helpfulness of the adjective is, in any case, debatable.)

Those who write on the subject frequently refer to the need for 'trust' and seem to imply that this somehow ought to be present. The conference poses real problems in this respect which it is necessary to face. In the presence of a group, not all of whose members know each other well (some indeed may never have met before) a degree of reserve or caution is appropriate. Especially at first time conferences, it is unrealistic to expect full and frank communication. Participants will exercise proper restraint until they are better acquainted. In view of the constant emphasis on the need for divulging detailed information as quickly as possible when urgent case conferences are called, it may seem that this is a fundamental contradiction of the conference purpose and such reticence invalidates the aim of the conference. In our view, there is no way in which this tension can be eliminated, but the way in which sensitive material is used and the points at which a chairperson may draw attention to the confidentiality of certain matters in particular may go some way to relieve realistic concern.

There are particular difficulties for some professionals if the conference decision is paving the way for a court case. We have referred earlier to the health visitor who was deliberately reticent (we learnt afterwards) because she feared the information provided to the case conference might result in her being subpoenaed. Reluctance to appear voluntarily in court may spring from a fear that voluntary disclosure of information in such situations will result in irreparable damage to the relationship with the patient. This is of course a concern which is shared by others, especially GPs. Continuing contact with a family after a court appearance depends on many factors. Whether or not the case is successful, linked to the extent to which the parents admit guilt, will produce a wide variety of reactions in parents to those who have previously sought to help them in one way or another. The degree of authority carried by the particular professional will be relevant in gaining access, although this by itself is of little value in continuing work with the family. The need of the family for the services which a particular professional can offer is clearly another consideration and in this a GP may, for example, be more readily perceived by the family as of continuing value than a health visitor. But the relationship which any of the professionals builds up and the way in which they handle this after a court appearance will probably be a decisive factor in establishing a continuing link. Thus, although social workers may carry more authority in some respects, for example, when a supervision order is in force, it is not correct to suggest, as did some of our respondents, that social workers have 'a right of entry', whereas health visitors do not.

The issue of confidentiality presents moral and practical dilemmas to those participating in case conferences. While these dilemmas should not be minimised, it should also be acknowledged that the principle of confidentiality may be used as an excuse for withholding information when, in fact, other less acceptable motives are in operation. One of these is power, both personal and professional. On occasions, workers may experience a sense of personal power by keeping back what they know. (Keeping secrets is a well-known childhood game used to infuriate others.) Professional power may be a disguised version of this, part of the mystique to which organisational rivalries are added.

Sadly, we must also now take into account the anxiety and guilt which may cause participants to hold back contributions which might call in question their handling of the case. Where emotional involvement with particular family members is too intense, disclosure may also be difficult. In both situations, more often it is not deliberate or conscious withholding but a matter of selective reporting, 'forgetting', or playing down that which is, for one reason or another, difficult for the participant to face openly.

To acknowledge the complicated inter-actions, which are involved in decisions apparently about confidentiality, is not to minimise the widespread concern in society lest information provided for one purpose be used for other less desirable ends. Even within the framework of health and personal social services this is a matter about which there has to be vigilance, especially since it is sometimes difficult to disentangle the benefits and 'disbenefits' to clients of such sharing. Our earlier discussion of conference recording is particularly pertinent here, since the written record and its dissemination raises most anxiety about the protection of the individual's rights to privacy.

In any discussion, therefore, of confidentiality its central place in professional ethics and social values, as well as its rhetorical usage as a smoke screen for other problems of co-operation, must be taken into account. Exhortations to behave as if internal constraints or forces were not at work are pointless. All those who work together at conferences, but above all the chairperson, have to take account of real and apparent objections to sharing and to find ways of both resolving genuine ethical dilemmas and clearing away the smoke, which may be used to obscure the crucial issues involved in professional communication.

Chapter 5

Conclusion

We hope that this book will be regarded as an introduction to a subject of considerable significance to the helping professions. It is introductory in two senses. First, the evidence from empirical research contained within it is slight. Our own case conference study was modest in its purpose and scale and other work, although valuable, has scarcely begun to mine a rich field of study concerned with the attitudes of professionals to each other and their practice so far as communication and co-operation are concerned.

Secondly, we chose to focus upon child abuse and neglect for this discussion about interprofessional work when the issue has much wider implications. This was not arbitrary, for child abuse and neglect has roused public and professional concern and anxiety to an extent hitherto unknown amongst social workers and perhaps also amongst some others in the helping professions, especially health visitors. As we have discussed, this has led to advice, guidance and instruction to professionals from both central and local government on an unprecedented scale. This may be compared to the legislation and subsequent statutory instruments concerning children in care, which were in part a response to the tragedy of the Denis O'Neill case (Cmnd 6636, 1945). But the official response to the Maria Colwell inquiry, and the events which followed it, have demonstrated over four years a continuing preoccupation, expressed through the setting up of inquiries and a succession of memoranda, which shows no sign of abating. It seemed useful, therefore, to discuss the problems which arise when professionals work together (or are exhorted to do so) in this specific context. It is one which would be readily accepted as important, and it raises certain interesting and unusual features, for example, the extent to which people, whose working lives do not otherwise bring them in contact, are perforce drawn together to discuss this problem.

However, it is obviously important for the theme of interprofessional work to be studied across a range of client groups and problems, and many of the matters which we raise are relevant to these. For example, juvenile delinquency and mental and physical handicap raise similar crucial questions. A case could be made out for these and many other areas to be studied in depth. But we would argue that priority should be given next to the elderly, with especial reference to the inter-action of income maintenance, housing, health and personal social services. This is partly a simple question of numbers. We know that the population of the frail elderly will greatly increase in the next twenty years and that to care for them appropriately will be costly and complicated. It is also obvious that effective co-operation between these services is essential because the needs of the elderly, physical, environmental and social, are inextricably intertwined. Whilst this is true to an extent for all of us, the consequences of the health problems of the frail elderly for social care make the need to achieve effective co-operation especially important. Furthermore, the relationship between hospital care and that offered by residential homes opens up a whole new dimension of co-operation (or lack of it) not touched upon in this book.

Another aspect of this issue, so important for the well-being of many citizens, concerns professional education. We have discussed, albeit tentatively, some of the attitudes and values which different occupational groups bring to their work and the frames of reference with which they approach it. Education and training play key roles in shaping all these. The question must, therefore, arise as to whether some forms of shared education would facilitate better working relationships. At what stage and in what form such educational experiences should be available is not as yet clear and there is an urgent need for some closely monitored experiments. Even without shared teaching, however, which poses formidable organisational problems, much more could be done by the different professions in opening up for their students an informed debate about their future partners in social care. They need to discuss the implications of the inescapable fact that working well with others is a crucial element in their professional competence. We hope this book will stimulate further thought and innovation on this matter.

References

Anderson, M. (1977), 'An obstetrician's view', in Franklin (ed.), *Child Abuse—Prediction, Prevention and Follow-Up*, pp. 85-9.

Atkinson, P. (1977), 'The reproduction of medical knowledge', in Dingwall *et al.* (eds), op. cit.

Auckland Report (1975), *Report of the Committee of Inquiry into the Provision and Co-ordination of Services to the Family of John George Auckland*, DHSS (London: HMSO).

Baher, E., Hyman, C., Jones, C., Jones, R., Kerr, A., and Mitchell, R. (1976), *At Risk: An Account of the Work of the Battered Child Research Department, NSPCC* (London: Routledge & Kegan Paul).

Banta, H. D., and Fox, R. C. (1972), 'Role strains of a health care team in a poverty community', *Social Science and Medicine*, vol. 6, pp. 697-722.

Bartlett, H. M. (1970), *The Common Base of Social Work Practice* (New York: National Association of Social Workers).

BASW (British Association of Social Workers) (1977), *The Social Work Task*, a BASW Working Party Report (Birmingham: BASW Publications).

BASW (1978), *The Central Child Abuse Register*, a BASW Working Party Report (Birmingham: BASW Publications).

Becker, H. S., Geer, B., Hughes, E. C., and Strauss, A. L. (1961), *Boys in White* (Chicago: University of Chicago Press).

Beer, S. (1975), 'A medical social worker's view', in Franklin (ed.), *Concerning Child Abuse*, pp. 73-7.

Bell, N. W., and Vogel, E. F. (eds) (1960), *A Modern Introduction to the Family* (New York: The Free Press).

Bennett, P., Dawar, A., and Dick, A. (1972), 'Interprofessional co-operation', *Journal of the Royal College of General Practitioners*, vol. 22, pp. 603-9.

Berkowitz, L. (1965), *Advances in Experimental Psychology*, Vol. 2 (London and New York: Academic Press).

Berkowitz, L. (1953), 'Sharing leadership in small, decision-making groups', *Journal of Abnormal Psychology*, no. 48, pp. 231-8.

Beswick, K. (1977), 'Prediction and prevention in general practice', in Franklin (ed.), *Child Abuse—Prediction, Prevention and Follow-Up*, pp. 101-5

Bevan, H. (1975), 'Should reporting be mandatory?', in Franklin (ed.), *Concerning Child Abuse*, pp. 133-5.

Boyle, C. M. (1975), 'Differences between patients' and doctors' interpretations of some common medical terms', in Cox and Mead (eds), op. cit.

Brown, R. G. S. (1975), *The Management of Welfare* (Glasgow: Fontana).

Brown, J., and Howes, G. (eds) (1975), *The Police and the Community* (Westmead, Hants: Saxon House).

Butrym, Z. (1976), *The Nature of Social Work* (London: Macmillan).

Carter, J. (1976), 'Co-ordination and child abuse', *Social Work Service*, no. 9, pp. 22-8.

Carter, J. (1977), 'Is child abuse a crime?', in Franklin (ed.), *The Challenge of Child Abuse*, pp. 200-5.

Castle, R. L. (1976), *Case conferences: a cause for concern?* (London: NSPCC National Advisory Centre on the Battered Child).

Castle, R. L., and Kerr, A. M. (1972), *A Study of Suspected Child Abuse* (London: NSPCC).

CCETSW (Central Council for Education and Training in Social Work) (1976), *Values in Social Work* (London: CCETSW Paper 13).

CETHV (Council for the Education and Training of Health Visitors) (1965), *The Function of the Health Visitor* (London: CETHV).

Collie, J. (1975), 'The police role', in Franklin (ed.), *Concerning Child Abuse*, pp. 123-6.

Colwell Report (1974), *Report of the Committee of Inquiry into the Care and Supervision Provided in Relation to Maria Colwell*, DHSS (London: HMSO).

Cmnd 6636 (1945), *Report by Sir Walter Monckton on the circumstances which led to the boarding out of Denis and Terence O'Neill at Bank Farm, Minsterley, and the steps taken to supervise their welfare* (London: HMSO).

Cmnd 3569 (1968), *Royal Commission on Medical Education* (Todd Report) (London: HMSO).

Cmnd 3703 (1968), *Report of the Committee on Local Authority and Allied Personal Social Services* (Seebohm Report) (London: HMSO).

Cmnd 6684 (1976), *Fit for the Future* (Court Report) (London: HMSO).

Cmnd 7123 (1978), *Violence to Children: A Response to the First Report from the Select Committee on Violence in the Family* (London: HMSO).

Cooper, C. (1977), 'Preparing the paediatrician's evidence in care proceedings', Franklin (ed.), *Child Abuse—Prediction, Prevention and Follow-Up*, pp. 157-60.

Cox, C., and Mead, A. (eds) (1975), *A Sociology of Medical Practice* (London: Collier-Macmillan).

Craft, M., and Craft, A. (1971), 'The interprofessional perspectives of teachers and social workers: a pilot inquiry', *Social and Economic Administration*, vol. 5, no. 1, pp. 19-28.

Creighton, S. J., and Owtram, P. J. (1977), *Child Victims of Physical Abuse: A Report on the Findings of NSPCC Special Units' Registers* (London: NSPCC).

Davidson, S. (1976), 'Planning and co-ordination of social services in multi-organisational contexts', *Social Service Review*, vol. 50, no. 1, pp. 117-37.

Davie, R. (1977), 'The interface between education and social services', in DHSS, *Working Together for Children and Their Families*, pp. 46-52.

Davies, J. M. (1975), 'A health visitor's viewpoint', in Franklin (ed.), *Concerning Child Abuse*, pp. 78-81.

Davies, M. (1969), *Probationers and their Social Environment* (London: HMSO).

Davis, F. (1975), 'Professional socialisation as subjective experience: the process of doctrinal conversion among student nurses', in Cox and Mead (eds), op. cit., pp. 116-31.

Dear, G. (1975), 'The future development of police organisation', in Brown and Howes (eds), op. cit., pp. 31-9.

Desborough, C., and Stevenson, O. (1977), *Case Conferences: A Study of Interprofessional Communication Concerning Children At Risk* (University of Keele: Social Work Research Project).

DHSS and Home Office (1970), *Battered Babies*, Letter CMO 2/70.

DHSS (1972), *Battered Babies*, Letter LASSL(26)72.

DHSS (1974), *Non-Accidental Injury to Children*, Letter LASSL (74)13.

DHSS (1975), *Non-accidental injury to children: proceedings of a conference held at the DHSS on 19 June 1974* (London: HMSO).

DHSS (1976a), *Non-Accidental Injury to Children: Area Review Committees*, Letter LASSL(76)2.

DHSS (1976b), *Priorities for Health and Personal Social Services in England—A Consultative Document* (London: HMSO).

DHSS and Home Office (1976), *Non-Accidental Injury to Children: The Police and Case Conferences*, Letter LASSL(76)26.

DHSS Welsh Office (1977), *Working Together for Children and Their Families* (London: HMSO).

DHSS (Social Work Research Project) (1978), *Social Service Teams: The Practitioner's View* (London: HMSO).

Dingwall, R. (1977), *The Social Organisation of Health Visitor Training* (London: Croom Helm).

Dingwall, R. (1978), 'Problems of teamwork in primary care', paper presented to Personal Social Services Council Seminar on 'Teamwork'. (Available from: Centre for Socio-Legal Studies, Wolfson College, Oxford.)

Dingwall, R., Heath, C., Reid, M., and Stacey, M. (eds) (1977), *Health Care and Health Knowledge* (London: Croom Helm).

Dingwall, R., and McIntosh, J., 'Teamwork in theory and practice', in Dingwall and McIntosh (eds), op. cit., pp. 118-34.

Dingwall, R., and McIntosh, J. (eds) (1978), *Readings in the Sociology of Nursing* (Edinburgh: Churchill Livingstone).

Drake, F. (1975), 'The position of the local authority', in Franklin (ed.), *Concerning Child Abuse*, pp. 85-94.

East Sussex County Council (1975), *Children at Risk* (East Sussex County Council). (Available from: Pelham House, St Andrew's Lane, Lewes, East Sussex.)

Etzioni, A. (ed.) (1969), *The Semi-Professions and their Organisation* (New York: The Free Press).

Evans, N. (1977), 'The professional stance of teachers', in DHSS, op. cit., pp. 97-104.

Fitzherbert, K. (1977), *Child Care Services and the Teacher* (London: Temple Smith).

Franklin, A. W. (ed.) (1975), *Concerning Child Abuse* (Edinburgh: Churchill Livingstone).

Franklin, A. W. (ed.) (1977a), *Child Abuse—Prediction, Prevention and Follow-Up* (Edinburgh: Churchill Livingstone).

Franklin, A. W. (ed.) (1977b), *The Challenge of Child Abuse* (London: Academic Press).

Freidson, E. (1975), 'Dilemmas in the doctor/patient relationship', in Cox and Mead (eds), op. cit., pp. 285-98.

Gelles, C. A., and Gelles, M. (1975), 'The social construction of child abuse', *American Journal of Orthopsychiatry*, vol. 45, no. 363.

Gil, D. (1970), *Violence Against Children* (Cambridge, Mass.: Harvard University Press).

Goldberg, E. M. (1970), *Helping the Aged* (London: Allen & Unwin).

Goldberg, E. M., and Neill, J. E. (1972), *Social Work in General Practice* (London: Allen & Unwin).

Goldberg, E. M., Warburton, R. W., McGuiness, B., and Rowlands, J. (1977), 'Towards accountability in social work: one year's intake to an area office', *British Journal of Social Work*, vol. 7, no. 3, pp. 257-83.

Goldstein, H. (1973), *Social Work Practice: A Unitary Approach* (New York: Columbia University Press).

Goldstein, J., Freud, A., and Solnit, A. J. (1973), *Beyond the Best Interests of the Child* (London: Collier-Macmillan).

Goodman, L. (1975), 'Aspects of law in relation to non-accidental injury to children', in DHSS, op. cit., pp. 34-42.

Grey, E. (1969), *Workloads in Children's Departments* (London: HMSO).

Hall, M. H. (1975), 'A view from the emergency and accident department', in Franklin (ed.), *Concerning Child Abuse*, pp. 7-20.

Halsey, A. H. (1972), *Educational Priority* (London: HMSO).

Hart, M. H. (1978), *Teachers and Social Workers: A Case Study of Inter-professional Relationships* (unpublished MA thesis, University of Manchester).

HC 329 (1977), *First Report from the Select Committee on Violence in the Family, Session 1976-77: Violence to Children*, Vol. I Report (together with the Proceedings of the Committee), Vol. II Evidence, Vol. III Appendices (London: HMSO).

HC 506 (1977), *Children in Care in England and Wales, March 1976* (London: HMSO).

Helfer, R. E. (1968), 'The responsibility and role of the physician', in Helfer and Kempe (eds), op. cit., pp. 25-40; also in 2nd edn, 1974.

Helfer, R. E., and Kempe, C. H. (eds (1968), *The Battered Child* (Chicago: University of Chicago Press)..

Helfer, R. E., and Kempe, C. H. (eds) (1976), *Child Abuse and Neglect: The Family and the Community* (Cambridge, Mass.: Ballinger).

Heslin, R., and Dunphy, D. (1964), 'Three dimensions of member satisfaction in small groups', *Human Relations*, no. 17, pp. 99-112.

Hill, M. J. (1972), *The Sociology of Public Administration* (London: Weidenfeld & Nicolson).

Hill, M. J., and Laing, P. (1979), *Social Work and Money* (London: Allen & Unwin).

Hoffman, L. R. (1965), 'Group problem solving', in Berkowitz (ed.), op. cit., pp. 99-132.

Home Office (1950) (Joint Circular with Ministry of Health and Ministry of Education), *Children Neglected or Ill-treated in their own Homes* (London: HMSO).

Jefferys, M. (1965), *An Anatomy of Social Welfare Services* (London: Michael Joseph).

Jones, D. N., McClean, R., and Vobe, R. (1978), *Case Conferences on Child Abuse: The Nottinghamshire Approach* (unpublished paper submitted to the Second International Congress on Child Abuse and Neglect, London).

Kahn, A. J. (1974), 'Institutional constraints to interprofessional practice', in Rehr (ed.), op. cit., pp. 14-25.

Kane, R. A. (1975), *Interprofessional Teamwork* (Syracuse: Syracuse University School of Social Work, Manpower Monograph No. 8).

Karen Spencer Report (1978), *Report of Professor J. D. McClean concerning Karen Spencer to the Derbyshire County Council and Derbyshire Area Health Authority* (Derbyshire County Council).

Kellmer-Pringle, M. (1975), *The Needs of Children* (London: Hutchinson).

Kempe, C. H., Silverman, F. N., Steele, B. F., Droegmueller, W., and Silver, H. K. (1962), 'The battered child syndrome', *Journal of the American Medical Association*, vol. 181, no. 17.

Kempe, C. H., and Helfer, R. E. (eds) (1972), *Helping the Battered Child and his Family* (Philadelphia: Lippincott).

Kempe, R. S., and Kempe, C. H. (1978), *Child Abuse* (London: Fontana/Open Books).

Kilby, R., and Constable, T. (1975), 'The police and social workers', in Brown and Howes (eds), op. cit., pp. 47-55.

Lisa Godfrey Report (1975), *Report of the Joint Committee of Inquiry into Non-Accidental Injury to Children with particular reference to the case of Lisa Godfrey* (London: Lambeth, Southwark and Lewisham Area Health Authority (Teaching) and London Boroughs of Lambeth, Southwark and Lewisham).

Lishman, J. (1978), 'A clash in perspective? A study of worker and client perceptions of social work', *British Journal of Social Work*, vol. 8, no. 3, pp. 301-11.

Lupton, G. C. M. (1977), 'Area review committees', in Franklin (ed.), *Child Abuse—Prediction, Prevention and Follow-Up*, pp. 141-4.

Lynch, M. (1976), 'Risk factors in the child: a study of abused children and their siblings', in *The Abused Child*, ed. H. Martin (Cambridge, Mass.: Ballinger).

Martin, H. P. (1977), 'A child oriented approach to prevention of abuse', in Franklin (ed.), *Child Abuse—Prediction, Prevention and Follow-Up*, pp. 9-19.

Mayer, J. E., and Timms, N. (1970), *The Client Speaks* (London: Routledge & Kegan Paul).

McLeod, D. L., and Meyer, H. J. (1967), 'A study of the values of social workers', in Thomas (ed.), op. cit., pp. 401-6.

Menzies, I. (1970), *The Functioning of Social Systems as a Defence against Anxiety* (London: Tavistock Institute of Human Relations).

Meyer, H. J., Likwak, E., and Warren, E. (1968), 'Occupational and class differences in social values: a comparison of teachers and social workers', *Sociology of Education*, vol. 41, no. 3, pp. 263-81.

Mounsey, J. (1975), 'Offences of criminal violence, cruelty and neglect against children in Lancashire', in Franklin (ed.), *Concerning Child Abuse*, pp. 127-30.

Okell Jones, C. (1977), 'Development of children from abusive families', in Franklin (ed.), *Child Abuse—Prediction, Prevention and Follow-Up*, pp. 61-70.

Oliver, J. (1975), 'Some studies of families in which children suffer maltreatment', in Franklin (ed.), *The Challenge of Child Abuse*, pp. 16-37.

Olsen, K., and Olsen, M. (1967), 'Role expectations and perceptions for social workers in medical settings', *Social Work*, vol. 12, pp. 70-8.

Oppé, T. E. (1975), 'Problems of communication and co-ordination', in Franklin (ed.), *Concerning Child Abuse*, pp. 155-61.

Ounsted, C., Oppenheimer, R., and Lindsay, J. (1975), 'The psychopathology and psychotherapy of the families: aspects of bonding failure', in Franklin (ed.), *Concerning Child Abuse*, pp. 30-40.

Pföhl, S. J. (1977), 'The "discovery" of child abuse', *Social Problems*, vol. 24, no. 3, pp. 310-23.

Pincus, A., and Minahan, A. (1973), *Social Work Practice: Model and Method* (Illinois: Peacock).

Prins, H. A., and Whyte, M. B. H. (1972), *Social Work and Medical Practice* (Oxford: Pergamon Press).

Rapoport, R. N. (1960), *Community as Doctor* (London: Tavistock).

Regensburg, J. (1974), 'A venture in interprofessional discussion', in Rehr (ed.), op. cit., pp. 35-73.

Rehr, H. (ed.) (1974), *Medicine and Social Work: An Exploration in Interprofessionalism* (New York: Prodist).

Reid, W. (1964), 'Inter-agency co-ordination in delinquency and control', *Social Services Review*, vol. XXXVIII, no. 4, pp. 418-28.

Reid, W. J., and Shyne, A. (1969), *Brief and Extended Casework* (New York: Columbia University Press).

Richards, M. (1975), 'Non-accidental injury to children in an ecological perspective', in DHSS, op. cit., pp. 5-12.

Robinson, M. (1978), *Schools and Social Work* (London: Routledge & Kegan Paul).

Rowe, J. (1977a), 'Alternative families', in Franklin (ed.), *The Challenge of Child Abuse*, pp. 145-60.

Rowe, J. (1977b), in HC 329-II, p. 556.

Rowe, J., and Lambert, L. (1973), *Children Who Wait—A Study of Children Needing Substitute Parents* (London: British Association of Adoption Agencies).

Rubin, I. M., Plovnick, M. S., and Fry, R. E. (1975), *Improving the Co-ordination of Care: A Program for Health Team Development* (Cambridge, Mass.: Ballinger).

114   *Child Abuse*

Schmitt, B. D. (ed.) (1978), *The Child Protection Team Handbook* (New York: Garland, STPM Press).

Simon Peacock Report (1978), *Report of the Committee of Enquiry Concerning Simon Peacock* (Cambridgeshire County Council).

Simpson, R. L., and Simpson, I. H. (1969), 'Women and bureaucracy in the semi-professions', in Etzioni (ed.), op. cit., pp. 196-265.

Skinner, A. E., and Castle, R. L. (1969), *78 Battered Children: A Retrospective Study* (London: NSPCC).

Steven Meurs Report (1975), *Report of the Review Body Appointed to Enquire into the Case of Steven Meurs* (Norfolk County Council).

Stevenson, O. (1963), 'Co-ordination reviewed', in *Social Work and Social Values*, ed. E. Younghusband (London: Allen & Unwin, 1967), pp. 113-20, reprinted from *Case Conference*, vol. IX, no. 8, February 1963.

Stevenson, O. (1973), *Claimant or Client?* (London: Allen & Unwin).

Stone, R. (1977), 'General practitioners and child abuse', in Franklin (ed.), *Child Abuse—Prediction, Prevention and Follow-Up*, pp. 106-10.

Stroud, J. (1975), 'The social worker's role', in Franklin (ed.), *Concerning Child Abuse*, pp. 95-105.

Thomas, E. J. (ed.) (1967), *Behavioural Science for Social Workers* (New York: The Free Press).

Tibbits, J. (1975), 'Punishment, retribution and rehabilitation', in Franklin (ed.), *The Challenge of Child Abuse*, pp. 183-91.

Tibbitt, J. (1975), *The Social Work/Medicine Interface: A Review of Research* (unpublished paper, Social Work Services Group, Scottish Education Department).

Till, K., 'A neurosurgeon's viewpoint' in Franklin (ed.), *Concerning Child Abuse*, pp. 56-62.

Toren, N. (1969), 'Semi-professionalism and social work: a theoretical perspective', in Etzioni (ed.), op. cit., pp. 141-95.

Utting, W. (1978), 'The role of the Social Work Service of DHSS', *Social Work Service*, no. 16, pp. 1-13.

Wayne Brewer Report (1977), *Report of the Review Panel Appointed by the Somerset Area Review Committee to Consider the Case of Wayne Brewer*, (Somerset County Council and Somerset Area Health Authority).

Webb, A. L. (1975), *Co-ordination between Health and Personal Social Services: A Question of Quality* (unpublished paper presented to European Seminar on Interaction of Social Welfare and Health Personnel in the Delivery of Services: Implications for Training).

Webb, Dom B. (1975), 'Strengthening the individual', in Franklin (ed.), *The Challenge of Child Abuse*, pp. 229-40.

Wedlake, M. (1977), 'A police view of the present position', in Franklin (ed.), *Child Abuse—Prediction, Prevention and Follow-Up*, pp. 126-9.

Wootton, B. (1959), *Social Science and Social Pathology* (London: Allen & Unwin).

Wootton, B. (1978), 'The social work task today', *Community Care*, no. 233, pp. 14-16.

Younghusband, E. (1978), *Social Work in Britain: 1950-1975. A Follow-up Study*, Vols I and II.

Index

Adoption 54-6
administration 21
Anderson, M. 32
anxiety: high level of in cases of child abuse 15-16, 20; and publicity 56; sharing and diffusing of 64-5, 77-9
area health authorities 2
area review committees 4-7, 18, 43, 60-1
assault, legal definition of 39
Atkinson, P. 33
Auckland Report 1, 2-3, 32, 56

Baker, E. 19
Banta, H. D. 26
Bartlett, H. M. 50
'battered babies' 3
Becker, H. S. 25, 34
Beer, S. 53
Bell, N. W. 68
Bennett, P. 29
Berkowitz, L. 86
Beswick, K. 37, 38
Bevan, H. 102-3
bonding 72, 73, 90
Boyle, C. M. 47
Brewer, Wayne 61-2
British Association of Social Workers 7, 8, 10, 51, 63-4
British Paediatric Association 3, 63-4
Brown, J. 22
Brown, R. G. S. 5
bureaucracy 12-13
Butrym, Z. 50

Care orders: number made 16-17; decisions on 54-6, 65; and place of safety orders 88-9
Carter, J. 3, 38
case conferences: number held 16; doctors as participants in 33-4, 35-6; police as participants in 39, 43-4; timing of 40-1, 60; expectations of 57; history 58-9; decision to call 61-3; purposes of 63-5; sharing information at 65-73; decision-making at 73-6; and legal proceedings 76-7; sharing anxiety at 77-9; dynamics of 80-7; communication in

case conferences, cont.,
87-91; chairing of 91-6; length of 95; preliminary work for 96-7; minutes 97-9; and confidentiality 99-105
Castle, R. L. 30, 38, 70, 92
Central Council for Education and Training in Social Work 51
chairpersons 58, 78, 88, 90, 91-6
child abuse: definition xii, 45; co-ordinating committees on 1; co-ordination between welfare agencies 3; public awareness of 16, 106; role of health visitors 29-30; 'syndrome' 33; cases referred by GP's 33, 38; proportion of hospital admissions 34-5; criminal law on 38-9; role of teachers 45-7, 70; role of social workers 47-56; and family history 67-8, 72; attitudes to 81-2; predictors and signs of 89-91
children at risk: registers of 4-5, 8-11, 64, 65, 74; siblings of 68
children's homes 58
Chronically Sick and Disabled Persons Act 48
civil liberties 9
Collie, J. 39, 42
Colwell Report xi; on Seebohm 2; and place of safety orders 17; on making records 41, 43; on role of teachers 45, 47, 70; and publicity 56; on inter-professional communication 57, 99-100, 106
confidentiality 37, 99-105
Constable, T. 23
Cooper, C. 35, 36, 54
Craft, M. and A. 46
Creighton, S. J. 44-5
criminal law 38-9

Davidson, S. 5-6
Davie, R. 12
Davies, J. M. 53
Davies, M. 50
Dear, G. 39
Defence, Ministry of 44
denial 82
diagnosis 8